A RESTLESS PAST

A Restless Past

HISTORY AND THE AMERICAN PUBLIC

JOYCE APPLEBY

ROWMAN & LITTLEFIELD PUBLISHERS, INC.
Lanham • Boulder • New York • Toronto • Plymouth, UK

ROWMAN & LITTLEFIELD PUBLISHERS, INC.

Published in the United States of America
by Rowman & Littlefield Publishers, Inc.
A wholly owned subsidiary of The Rowman & Littlefield Publishing Group, Inc.
4501 Forbes Boulevard, Suite 200, Lanham, Maryland 20706
www.rowmanlittlefield.com

Estover Road
Plymouth PL6 7PY
United Kingdom

British Library Cataloguing in Publication Information Available

The hardback edition of this book was previously catalogued by the Library of Congress as follows:

Appleby, Joyce Oldham.
    A restless past : history and the American public / Joyce Oldham Appleby.
       p. cm.
    Includes bibliographical references and index.
       1. United States—Historiography. 2. Historiography—Social aspects—United   States. 3.
Historiography—Political aspects—United States. 4. United
States—History—Philosophy. I. Title.

  E175.A668 2004
  973.4'072—dc22   2004017213

ISBN-10 : 0-7425-4252-1 (cloth : alk. paper)
ISBN-13 : 978-0-7425-4252-5 (cloth : alk. paper)
ISBN-10 : 0-7425-4253-X (pbk : alk. paper)
ISBN-13 : 978-0-7425-4253-2 (pbk : alk. paper)

Printed in the United States of America

To the future and my grandchildren:
Hannah Marion Lansburgh, Flora Ann Lansburgh,
John Lansburgh Caylor, and Andrew Bergmann Caylor

CONTENTS

INTRODUCTION

Over the past decade and a half, the American public has developed a contentious relationship with historians, if not history itself. During this time, commemorative events became battlefields of contested meanings. New narrative accounts provoked arguments about what the United States should stand for. Within the academy, postmodernist skepticism about the very idea of objectivity further roiled the waters. The end of the Cold War made it possible for historians to think beyond nations as the natural units of historical analysis. Curiosity about diverse cultures and the way in which cultural influences shape the way people perceive their world acted like a lever under unexamined assumptions about the existence of universal human qualities that historians shared with most of the public. These fresh perspectives have shattered conventional ways of thinking, making this an exhilarating time to be a historian. They have also left historians with the challenge—even obligation—of engaging with the general public. In the articles, lectures, and presidential addresses gathered into this book, I examine these changes and the controversies they provoked. History plays a critical role in the United States where our shared sense of national values depends on our understanding of our nation's past.

Many of our contemporary battles over history can be traced to the 1960s, when a new cohort of students entered graduate school. America's universities had opened their doors after World War II to veterans, most of them funded by the GI Bill. African Americans and the children of the immigrants from Italy, Greece, the Balkans, and Germany who had come to the United States at the turn of the twentieth century entered the academy, often as the first in their families to gain advanced degrees.

Women too sought careers as historians and museum curators. These newcomers to higher education brought with them novel questions that illuminated a whole different historical landscape. They wanted to know about ordinary people and sought to locate their own forebears in the America past, rather than spend their time studying the familiar WASP gentlemen and Midwest radicals whose exploits had filled the history books up until then. Their rallying cry became "history from the bottom up."

Historical inquiries "from the bottom up" couldn't be answered in the traditional way. Ordinary people by definition did not sit in Congress or the Oval Office, didn't lead armies or head diplomatic missions. What could possibly justify studying these undistinguished men and women with their humdrum lives and conventional opinions? The answer: the insatiable curiosity of a new cohort of young scholars determined to listen to the voices that had been silenced by elite indifference. Energized by their trailblazing ways, they wittingly—or unwittingly—opened up big questions. Defying their mentors' notions of the proper subject matter for historical investigation, they ended up rewriting American history and created a template for challenging nationalistic histories everywhere. What soon became apparent was how much popular emotion was tied up with the story of American success.

Those writing dissertations in the 1960s and 1970s churned out novel research agendas with great gusto, calculating geographic and social mobility; the mortality and fertility rates that determined the growth and decline of populations; the workday of the immigrant, the slave, the laboring man and woman; the strictures guiding marriage and patterns of inheritance. They even discovered scores of unsung heroes. In addressing these fresh topics, these newly minted historians turned to long-term data sets in county property records, church registers, city directories, and election rolls. They used computers and social scientific hypotheses to extract new material from these recondite sources. They didn't seek the unique, bur rather the norms that gave meaning to people's lives.

The innovative research of the 1960s and 1970s stood on its head the older standard of historical significance like the one that Carl Becker offered at the beginning of the century. Becker wrote a widely reprinted essay explaining that history did not include any fact about the past, but only those about significant events. In saying this, Becker was endorsing a hierarchy of knowledge that had prevailed from the beginning of historical writing. Significant events dealt with kings and armies, nation building, the doings of geniuses, international conflicts, and the creation of great works of art.[1] Eschewing this distinction, social historians showed how almost everything in the past possesses significance. Their findings complicated the context in which so-called significant developments unfold. Learning about the processes and patterns that controlled and directed ordinary lives gave access to the larger world in which singular persons made critical decisions. It also created powerful identities for those people on the bottom who had so long been ignored. Concrete details about the experiences of women, African Americans, America's many immigrant groups, and workers created a rich reservoir of stories that capsized the nation's conventional narrative. At the same time, they added an analytical bite to earlier generalizations about the structuring of society, opportunity, and political power.

The new research dramatically transformed our understanding of America's past, but not without arousing public indignation. Many readers greeted with suspicion the unfamiliar names they found in recent history books. "If these men and women really belong to the past why didn't we know that before?" was their implicit query. Critics labeled the new history revisionism, a pejorative term that suggests manipulation of old material rather than the acquisition of new knowledge. Here was a reaction that disclosed a perceptual gulf between practitioners of history and their audiences. A part of the public evidently looks upon historical knowledge as already known and hence fixed for all time. Yet fresh inquiries in history constantly expand what is known as they do in any other scholarly pursuit. This is difficult to accept if one thinks that the past itself exercises some power over historical investigators. In actuality, the past totally disappears with each passing minute, leaving behind only traces that will need to be reconstructed and interpreted later, if at all. Neither professional historians nor anyone else possesses a retrospective camera to capture what actually happened.

Historical knowledge comes not from remembering the past, but from taking questions to it. If no one inquires about a past event or development, it remains obscure. Large hunks of past experience go unresearched and hence unknown and will continue so until someone thinks to ask about them. These are unpalatable truths for those who want certitude about our knowledge of the past. Nothing could be more strikingly different from the reception of most advances in historical scholarship! And when those advances upset settled views that impinge on political sympathies, the reaction can be sulfurous.

In a backhanded way these responses to historical scholarship point up the importance accorded history. People want students to be able to remember the history that they were taught in school. Newspapers frequently run articles about how little young people know about the past. Has any reporter thought of investigating how much young people retain from their mathematics, literature, or physics classes? It's historical knowledge that counts because it is deemed essential to forming sound opinions and to behaving as responsible citizens. History plays an essential role as a unifier in the life of a nation, a role with unavoidable political overtones. It also shapes how people view the world and the differences they encounter when they leave their own boundaried lives.

Helpful to me in understanding why some Americans insist on a particular account of the nation's past—often a sanitized one evading unpleasant truths—were the words of the anthropologist Mary Douglas. She observed that "any institution that is going to keep its shape needs to control the memory of its members." Going on to explain what she meant, Douglas said that controlling memory involves getting people "to forget experiences incompatible with" the institution's righteous image and brings to mind "events which sustain the view that is complementary to itself."[2] If we think of pundits and public officials as gatekeepers of national memory, we can understand why the exploratory scholarship of the past forty years has put scholars on a collision course with those trying to keep the shape of the nation.

The spark for what, in retrospect, seems like a predictable explosion came in 1994 when a council of academic historians and history schoolteachers working with the American Historical Association and the Department of Education published the National History Standards. The standards offered guidelines for curriculum in the fifth, eighth, and eleventh grades. Their development had been part of a larger government initiative to improve American public education. Since the history standards included much of the new material on African Americans, women, immigrants, and laborers, it was bound to jar those who favored the old story line that emphasized national successes and the leaders who achieved them. Why did "the past" now contain material about the lives of undistinguished Americans or extraordinary but unfamiliar persons like Harriet Tubman, a self-liberating slave who became a leader in the underground railroad? Saying that they had always been there in the past but no one had thought to ask about them did not satisfy the critics, most of whom wanted only a celebratory history of the United States.

The brouhaha over the National History Standards actually was a tempest in a teapot. Some members of the press and Congress got excited for a while, but teachers and textbook publishers were thrilled to have the riches of four decades of research laid out for them. Although they had no authority to impose content on the public schools, the standards carried the imprimatur of the distinguished historians who had worked on them. Critics disappeared with the smoke from the battlefield, and Harriet Tubman and her previously unknown sisters and brothers stayed in the textbooks. So too did the multitudinous facts about population growth, immigration trends, slave statistics, women's lives, family practices, land systems, inheritance processes, and geographic and social mobility rates that had become the hallmark of the new social history.

But there was no escape from controversy. Commemorations, remembrances, and memorials came around year after year, and now they were fraught with tension because the unsung had been sung, injustices exhumed, and disconcerting facts publicized. They were more likely to produce discord than to honor a past event. In 1992 Native Americans protested the idea of marking "the discovery" of their land by a European during the quincentenary of Columbus's voyage. Even more dismaying, the public learned for the first time of the devastation wrought by the diseases that Europeans had brought with them to the New World. Isolated from the biological homogenizing that Africans, Asians, and Europeans had experienced through centuries of explorations, the indigenous population of the Western Hemisphere turned out to be tragically vulnerable to the smallpox, pleurisy, typhus, measles, and tuberculosis that the Conquistadors brought to the Western Hemisphere. Over the course of four centuries of contact up to 90 percent of all Indians— from the Andes to Alaska—died.

Members of the public had largely been unaware of work by historical demographers and epidemiologists that had documented the deaths of successive waves of native victims. And when they did hear about them, they sometimes reacted in anger at being robbed of the celebratory spirit of "in 1492, Columbus sailed the ocean blue." Some wanted to celebrate the 500th anniversary of Columbus's initial encounter in the New World and others to focus on the havoc wreaked on the Indian tribes of North and South America by European diseases.

What began as a commemoration of the historic joining of the Old and New Worlds precipitated the dissemination of the sobering facts about this unintentional genocide. Much the same thing happened with the 250th anniversary of the birth of Thomas Jefferson in 1993. In the intervening fifty years since the bicentennial of his birthday, historians had examined Jefferson's disappointing record on slavery. What might have been a simple tribute to the celebrated author of the Declaration of Independence became the platform for discussing the Founding Fathers and their moral entanglements as slaveholders. When I gave my inaugural lecture as Harmsworth professor at Oxford in 1991, I chose to talk about the complex legacy that Jefferson had left Americans.[3] Entitling my lecture "Without Resolution: The Jeffersonian Tension in American Nationalism," I thought that I placed Jefferson's career in a balanced historical context. Consequently I was startled when a member of the audience who indicated that he had admired my lecture told me, "I have always disliked Jefferson, and now you have shown me why."

The fiftieth anniversary of the end of World War II drew historians into a round of new conflicts about the historical record. A projected exhibition at the Smithsonian's National Air and Space Museum in Washington, D.C., of the *Enola Gay*, the B-29 Superfortress that dropped the first atomic bomb, caused a furor. Survivors and curators fought over how to commemorate simultaneously the American victory in World War II and the beginning of the atomic age. To grasp the compelling drama of the storm over the *Enola Gay*, one needs to keep in mind a moment in history from two perspectives. The first contained American soldiers, readied for an invasion, ecstatic with relief when their young lives were no longer at risk because the bombing had brought surrender; the second that of Japanese children incinerated as they walked to school through the streets of Hiroshima in August 1945. Impossible to reconcile, the Smithsonian finally shrank the exhibit to showing the fuselage of the plane, its cavernous interior, empty save for one bomb.

In December 2003, the Smithsonian planned to display the *Enola Gay* again, this time under the rubric of the "most sophisticated propeller-driven bomber of World War II." Historians objected to showing the plane without accompanying material on nuclear weaponry or the devastation wrought in Japan, so they organized a conference to focus the public's attention on the vexed history of this Smithsonian artifact.[4] Here, historians took the initiative, insisting on a full account of the dropping of the first atomic bomb in opposition to the evident determination of the National Air and Space Museum and its supporters in the Air Force Association to rid the plane of its awesome associations.

While words flew thick and fast over the *Enola Gay* exhibit in 1995, halfway around the world in Nagasaki, Japanese veterans formed the Citizens Association to Rectify the Nagasaki Atomic Bomb Museum in order to cleanse the museum's exhibit of any untoward pictures of Japanese aggression lest future generations come to believe that the United States had dropped the atomic bomb because Japan had done something wrong.[5] The veterans group, like protesters in America, had been aroused by the redesigning of the Nagasaki Museum to incorporate the dropping of the American atomic bomb on Japan into a fuller story of the lead-up to World War II in Asia. The Japanese have begun to discuss publicly the sensitive subjects of the invasion of Nanking, the attack on Pearl Harbor, the wartime impressment of Korean "comfort women," and the Bataan march, with predictable outrage from the keepers of "the shape" of the nation. One heroic Japanese historian, Saburo Ienaga, waged a sixty-year campaign against his country's textbooks for their insistent exclusion of material such as the Japanese invasion of Korea and Manchuria.

In Germany the forty-four-year division of the country after World War II powerfully affected how that war was "remembered." Public exposure of the Nazi death camps engaged the attention of West Germans, but in the East commemorations of the war highlighted the German invasion of the Soviet Union and the victory of socialist armies over fascist invaders, not the Holocaust. In defeat, both halves of prewar Germany assumed separate parts of blame for the war. After the reunification of Germany, this difference became apparent, vividly demonstrating how the presentation of a nation's past reflects its political alignments. History evidently is too important to leave to the historians or, more correctly, historians often act as members of a society first and scholars second.

Historians' activism has taken many forms. In 2002, when the public began hearing more and more of President George W. Bush's intention to invade Iraq, 1,100 historians signed a petition to Congress reminding that august body that the Constitution gave it alone the power and responsibility to declare war. Presenting the American Historians Petition to Congress on September 17, Constitution Day, a delegation of the signatories explained in press releases and interviews that it was only during the Cold War that the president had preempted Congress in this awesome responsibility. Not since December 8, 1941, had an American president gone to Congress to ask for a declaration of war. In the meantime, Americans had fought in surrogate wars, proxy wars, police actions, and United Nation interventions, but officially the term "war" had been avoided in part to evade this constitutional stricture. During the week that the petition received attention, a National Public Radio interviewer called me to ask querulously how it could be that until he read the historians' petition he had not known that Congress possessed this power. The petition reminded senators and representatives that "Congress has not asserted its authority to declare war for over half a century, leaving the president solely in control of war powers to the detriment of our democracy and in clear violation of the Constitution." Here the historians used their knowledge of American institutions to make known the amendment of the Constitution through consensual silence.[6]

In 2003, plans for a new exhibition center for the Liberty Bell in Philadelphia embroiled historians in another dispute with the sanitizers of the American past. The National Park Service disclosed plans to build the new center on the grounds of the Masters-Penn House, which had been home to a succession of slaveholding notables, including President George Washington. Recoiling at the dissonance between human bondage and the cause of liberty, the designers of the Independence National Historical Park excluded any mention of slavery from the projected exhibit. A group of historians, backed by key Philadelphians, the *Philadelphia Enquirer*, and eventually the top brass of the National Park Service, took action. They urged that the new center present the paradoxes, pain, and ambiguities of the mixed foundation of laws upholding slavery and a commitment to the proposition that "all men are created equal" at the creation of the United States.[7]

These incidents drive home Douglas's point that institutions that want to keep a particular shape, such as nations, need to control the memory of their members, an imperative that historians are strenuously combating. The recent leavening of heroes and success stories with the broader findings of historians still does not sit well with many public officials. In the past two years, laws and proposed legislation in Congress have stressed the need for returning to the teaching of "traditional" American history in the nation's public schools. Appropriations for graduate education have also been targeted. Other congressional bills have stressed the importance of investing the content of public school history courses with the values of Western civilization and its free institutions.[8] Officials around the world have long tried to suppress the memory of injustices, whitewashing their nation's records to preserve the "righteous image" that Douglas said sustains a country's complimentary view of itself. The official guardians of memory often think about history instrumentally. For them it serves as a handmaiden of patriotism by glorifying the nation's past; it shores up the status quo by excluding disconfirming narratives. With the pool of historical knowledge vastly enlarged to include the ugly parts of the past, officials are going to be hard-pressed to suppress research that complicates the story they want to tell.

Concerted action to use history to secure recognition of past wrongs is not likely to abate in the near future. Many rivulets of concern have created new rivers of confrontation. The massive campaign to embed an enduring memory of the Holocaust in museums in Europe, Israel, and the Americas has served as a template for other groups. The human rights movement, exemplified by the international Helsinki Accord, has made men and women everywhere acutely aware of their rights, among them the right to have their grievances aired. Commissions in Ireland, Argentina, and South Africa have inspired others seeking public exposure of disappearances, massacres, enslavement, and ethnic cleansings. Historians have served these causes well in their struggles against governments that show more interest in hiding than in exhibiting disturbing truths about the past. In fighting for an inclusive memory, historians have acted on their deepest convictions that history arouses curiosity about humanity, teaches the lessons of unexpected consequences, and fortifies the will to study life in all its complexity while helping those who study it to reject consoling simplifications. The study of history nurtures curiosity, hope, and a taste for comprehensive understandings.

In recent years, journalists, judges, historians, and the global media have supplied heft to efforts to secure reconciliation and reparation of past wrongs. Never has the power of historical knowledge been so evident. People who have been wronged remember the wrongs as oral traditions pass down through generations, but documented accounts persuade those who were not personally affected. Spain's Baltazar Garzon demonstrated the power of a world no longer tolerant of abuses of power by seeing that General Augusto Pinochet was put under house arrest when he visited Great Britain. Historical studies like Peter Kornbluh's *The Pinochet File: A Declassified Dossier on Atrocity and Accountability* have reignited debates on major issues such as the role of the United States in the overthrow of Salvador Allende in Chile in 1973. Philip Dray's *At the Hands of Persons Unknown: The Lynching of Black America* helped revive a discussion on that shameful record, vivified by a powerful museum exhibition in 2002. After years of delay, the Smithsonian has begun work on a National Museum of African American History and Culture, a project started ninety years ago by black Civil War veterans.

The move for the recovery of memory is by no means confined to the United States. In Halabja, Iraq, the no-fly zone of the 1990s permitted Kurds to establish a museum featuring photographs of those killed in Saddam Hussein's aerial gas attacks on Kurdish villages in 1988. In Spain, a private initiative to locate the remains of Republicans executed during the Franco era led to an official recognition of the men and women who had suffered during the decades of repression. The Swiss legislature recently passed a resolution condemning Turkey's attacks on its Armenian population during World War I. And Nobel Peace Prize winner Rigoberta Menchu brought to world attention the massacres of the indigenous Maya-Quiche population by the Guatemalan military dictatorship in the 1980s.

The popularity of commemorations, memorials, and exhibitions, evident since the 1970s, has enhanced efforts to use history to validate claims for redress of past grievances. While the one effort is overtly political and the other academic, this use of history has made it the most politically powerful discipline in the humanities and social sciences. International tribunals are investigating claims of mass slaughters in

Guatemala, Bosnia, Rwanda, and Cambodia, with additional commissions in the planning stages.

Still another innovation in the presentation of historical material came from historians in the 1960s and 1970s who explored the dynamic between belief and behavior as a way of understanding how a given social consciousness emerged. Intellectual historians began to stress that society constructs reality for its members. They sought to discover the frames of reference, the unexamined assumptions, the cultural truths that formed what they called "the social construction of reality." This then became their focus of attention rather than the great ideas of an age. This innovative work occurred simultaneously with the effort of social historians to investigate the lives of ordinary people. Through this approach, they then challenged the patriotic view that the leaders of the American Revolution and the framers of the U.S. Constitution acted out of principles valid for all time. In the early twentieth century Progressive historians interpreted the Founders as moved by self-interest, but both principle and self-interest were congruent with the view that individuals were in charge of the contents of their mind instead of men and women being recipients of a worldview fashioned by their society before they were born.

The new emphasis highlighted how society propagates a particular system of beliefs that one learns as a child and continues to think within until death. Ideas, images, and truths were seen as so many building blocks in a structure of meaning expressed in shared assertions and underpinned by common assumptions. This concept of "ideology" began to replace "intellectual" in scholarly writings, signally a decisive shift away from the conviction that people's thinking was independent of the milieu in which they actually thought their thoughts.

With this notion of the social construction of reality, historians became less interested in the truth of any belief held by people in the past and more concerned to locate the force and effect of those beliefs. This ideological approach demanded that historians look at past situations the same way that contemporaries did in order to understand their motives for action rather than get outside of their world to judge them. Reasons replaced causes as the focus of historical interest; understandings became more important than the validity of any given belief. The concept of ideology helped early American historians comprehend why the colonists were so implacable in their resistance to the British imperial reforms that triggered the revolution. Later, they used it to good effect in interpreting the debates over the "more perfect union" created by the drafters of the U.S. Constitution.

I assessed the impact on colonial scholarship of both the new social history and the ideological approach to social thought in "A Different Kind of Independence: The Postwar Restructuring of the Historical Study of Early America."[9] Originally historians had construed the colonial period as the first chapter in the national epic, looking on all things colonial as seeds; more recently historians have studied the colonies as fascinating societies in themselves, their unique development often helping to answer larger questions about population growth, the impact of migration, and family structure in other seventeenth- and eighteenth-century European societies. European scholars opened up innovative lines of inquiry about agricultural changes and early industrialization, and early American historians began studying the colonies as different examples of modernizing societies. Unlike the proleptic approach of the patriotic interpretation, where only developments that could be seen as acorns for the great oak of the United States attracted interest, research on population dynamics, inheritance strategies, and community formation revealed how much the colonists had tried to replicate Old World traditions in their new communities, which in turn stimulated fresh interpretations of the Revolutionary era.

Looking at the act of nation building following the Revolution, my article entitled "The American Heritage: The Heirs and the Disinherited" addressed the wide-ranging debates about government and citizenship that preceded and followed the drafting of the United States Constitution.[10] Recognizing that it was during this period that Europeans came to see the United States as not only different, but exceptional, I took the theme of American exceptionalism for my presidential address for the Organization of American Historians, "Recovering America's Historic Diversity: Beyond Exceptionalism," included in this volume.[11]

The next three chapters in this volume address the impact of postmodernism on historical thought. Forming more of a cauldron of provocative ideas than a coherent intellectual position, postmodernists lobbed a heady load of criticism into the precincts of the humanities, principally those of literature, but also including history. They took on the objectivity of Western science, the stability of language, and the credibility of the individual consciousness, maintaining instead that objectivity was but a convenient fiction of Western culture, language a slippery medium of communication, and the heroic self a socially constructed "subject."[12]

Obsessed by the totalitarian aspect of social power, postmodernists embraced marginalized people and ideas in defiance of the established hierarchy of knowledge. As Pauline Rosenau amusingly summarized, they focused on "regions of resistance, the forgotten, the irrational, the insignificant, the repressed, the borderline, the classical, the sacred, the traditional, the eccentric, the sublimated, the subjugated, the rejected, the nonessential, the marginal, the peripheral, the excluded, the tenuous, the silenced, the accidental, the dispersed, the disqualified, the deferred, the disjointed—all that which 'the modern age' has never cared to understand in any particular detail, with any sort of specificity."[13] Here the postmodernist celebration of the marginalized echoed the earlier work of social historians who had devoted themselves to giving voice to the neglected. Cultural historians who have embraced many postmodern insights have also paid attention to the range of voices, signs, designs, and symbols that make up social communication. This stress on society's vast repertoire of communicative sounds and signs has made scholars aware of the different perspectives of the many participants to any event. It has also underscored the critical role of meaning in gauging why historical actors did what they did, moving away from the emphasis on cause that had previously engaged historians.

In "One Good Turns Deserves Another," I answer a postmodernist who argued for giving up on the chimera of neutral research in favor of playing with the words and witnesses the past has left us.[14] This recommendation to engage with the past rather than try to reconstruct what actually happened has had great appeal, in large part because of the recognition of the impossibility, as Michel Foucault put it, of representing an order of things through an order of words. Another response to this problem would be to abandon an outdated concept of objectivity and recognize that all knowledge begins inside someone's head with strong traces of the investigator's perspective. Questions and hypotheses drive scholarly work; assumptions, both recognized and unrecognized, influence all researchers. These givens do not eliminate the possibility of describing past events and developments with a high level of accuracy and comprehensiveness; they only qualify what we would call historical truth.

For American historians the most telling of postmodernists' critiques was their assault on the convictions promoted by Enlightenment figures whose assertions about human rights, nature, and progress had achieved iconic status in the United States. Totally dismissing the idea of universal principals, the postmodernists made salient (if only through the outrage their pronouncements evoked) the long shadow that the Enlightenment had cast on the United States. In contrast to the current emphasis on shifting meanings and slippery identities, those eighteenth-century savants stressed that truth and falsehood were stamped on the universe waiting for each investigator to discern. Truth for them came from the liberation of human reason. Thrilled by the formidable fortresses of knowledge that they were creating, the philosophes of the Enlightenment had few doubts about their scientific enterprises. Completely absent from their reflections was how passion, prejudice, or power might be influencing what was considered knowledge. Nor was there an awareness of the way that the Western emphasis on a particular kind of logical reasoning raised barriers to understanding the reasoning of non-Westerners. Where modern thinkers saw all investigations converging on verifiable conclusions, postmodernists saw inquiries merely proliferating. Truth and objectivity were out; meaning and perspective were in. "The Enlightenment Project in a Postmodernist Age" compares the central positions of the eighteenth-century reformers of the Enlightenment with their twentieth-century postmodernist critics.[15]

In the end, assertions about the unstable nature of language and representations through language had limited appeal. While most historians appreciate the difficulty of representing an order of things in an order of words, they proved reluctant to abandon all hope for objective reasoning about their research. Perhaps even more important, the postmodernists' insistence that the past is unknowable offered little help to those groups wishing to establish the authenticity of their accounts for purposes of reparation. Although the heyday of the postmodernist influence on historians has clearly passed, it's left an attitudinal legacy. Historians are now more aware of the construction of knowledge as a social enterprise in itself. Many have become attuned to the need to analyze symbols and words as social constructs. The voice of the omniscient historian so common in earlier histories, for example, "Napoleon marched his armies across the plains of Europe," has taken a backseat to the interpreter of past events who draws on diverse perspectives. The lofty, exterior explanations that once characterized historical writing now seems more like aspects of an imperialist enterprise than the voice of reason. I explore these labyrinthine paths that have carried scholars a long way away from the certitudes of a century ago in "The Power of History," an address I gave to the American Historical Association in 1997.[16]

The contested 2000 presidential election occasioned my participation in a forum that led to the writing of "Presidents, Congress, and Courts: Partisan Passions in Motion."[17] That pivotal event and the devastating attacks of September 11, 2001, demonstrated yet again how crises—particularly violent ones—make people cry out for explanations. They expose the layers of past experience that urgently need interpreting and push to the fore insistent questions about national purpose that lie dormant in normal times. The historian Daniel Boorstin said that to plan for the future without a sense of the past is like trying to plant cut flowers. When the unexpected destroys our constructed vision of the future that helps us move into it, historical knowledge can at least assure us that human societies have dealt with such crises before.

The occasion of my presidential address to the Society for Historians of the Early American Republic gave me a chance to talk about the ideological straitjacket in which historians have confined the subject of the market economy. In "The Vexed Story of Capitalism Told by American Historians" I make a plea for recognition of the great creative power of enterprise, especially in the United States. Capitalism, I argue, should be approached as both an economic system and a cultural force.[18] My appeal to culture conforms to the current tendency to use the shared symbols, myths, precepts, and teachings that we call culture to understand how society works. Since then culture has become so ubiquitous an explanation as to be analytically useless. Indeed, we are trapped between the undersocialized depiction of autonomous human beings of the Enlightenment and a concept of culture that leaves individuals with little personal force. Working out historical explanations between these two poles will be the challenge of the first quarter of the twenty-first century.

American historians have redefined what constitutes historical significance by studying the lives of ordinary people. At the same time, they have rejected the alignment of history with the explanatory model of the sciences. And they have broken out of an American frame of reference by following European scholarly leads after World War II. More recently, they have attended to the intellectual challenges thrown down by scholars outside the West. Having followed this survey of historical trends of the past fifteen years, a reader might be tempted to say that the more things change, the more they stay the same. Historical revisions and "new histories" seem always to be cropping up. It's certainly true that the Progressive historians of the early twentieth century became stormy petrels when they began their explorations of economic influences at play in the American Revolution, the drafting of the Constitution, and the Civil War. Charles Beard, Carl Becker, and their colleagues challenged the reigning, patriotic explanations of America's nation-building acts, but in other ways they reflected what Louis Hartz called "the limited social perspectives of the average American himself."[19]

That is far less true today, which is why there are tensions between professional historians and their public audiences. Concern about this demonstrates as nothing else could what a vital role history plays in the present. This is particularly true in the United States, which has depended critically on its national history to supply a coherent moral center of gravity to a citizenry of immigrants. In disputing what happened in the past, historians and members of the public are engaging in a serious intellectual enterprise to create a unifying account from a diversity of perspectives. Rising above the imperative phrased by Mary Douglas, they are groping with the idea that keeping the nation's shape involves more than suppressing the memory of shameful episodes in the past. Our past has been restless; we are restless about its representation. Accepting this restlessness comes with an honest effort to accept the frailties of our human natures without abandoning the nation's commitment to protecting liberty, human rights, and the search for truth.

NOTES

1. "What Are Historical Facts?" in *Detachment and the Writing of History* (1926; Ithaca, N.Y., 1955), 41–64.

2. Mary Douglas, *How Institutions Think* (Syracuse, 1982), 112.

3. *Without Resolution: The Jeffersonian Tension in American Nationalism*, Harmsworth Inaugural Lecture (Oxford, 1991). In 1998, DNA testing established that a Jefferson male had fathered Eston Hemings.

4. Debbie Ann Doyle, "Historians Protest New *Enola Gay* Exhibit," *Perspectives: Newsmagazine of the American Historical Association*, December 2003.

5. *New York Times*, July 4, 1996, A6.

6. "The Talk of the Town," *New Yorker*, September 30, 2002.

7. Gary Nash, "For Whom Will the Liberty Bill Toll? From Controversy to Collaboration," *George Wright Forum* 21 (2004).

8. Bruce Craig, "The Politics of 'Traditional' American History," *Perspectives: Newsmagazine of the American Historical Association*, November 2003.

9. *William and Mary Quarterly* 50 (April 1992).

10. *Journal of American History* 74 (December 1987).

11. "Recovering America's Historic Diversity: Beyond Exceptionalism" [presidential address to the Organization of American Historians], *Journal of American History* 79 (September 1992).

12. See Pauline Rosenau, *Post-modernism and the Social Sciences: Insights, Inroads, and Intrusions* (Princeton, 1991); and Joyce Appleby, Lynn Hunt, and Margaret Jacob, *Telling the Truth about History* (New York, 1994).

13. Rosenau, *Post-modernism and the Social Sciences*, 8.

14. "One Good Turn Deserves Another: A Response to David Harlan," *American Historical Review* 94 (December 1989).

15. "The Enlightenment Project in a Postmodernist Age," John R. Adams Lecture in Humanities, San Diego State University, November 21, 1994.

16. "The Power of History" [presidential address to the American Historical Association], *American Historical Review* 103 (February 1998).

17. *Journal of American History* 88 (2001).

18. "The Vexed Story of Capitalism Told by American Historians" [presidential address to the Society for Historians of the Early American Republic], *Journal of the Early Republic* 21 (2001).

19. *The Liberal Tradition in American History* (New York, 1955), 29.

1

WITHOUT RESOLUTION: THE JEFFERSONIAN TENSION IN AMERICAN NATIONALISM

Three presidential monuments grace the tidal basin of Washington, D.C.: the virile obelisk commemorating George Washington, the classical temple that encases a statue of Abraham Lincoln, and a lovely little rotunda honoring Thomas Jefferson. Washington, who bears the heavy burden of being the Father of his country, became a hallowed figure early in the history of the United States and remains the country's most respected hero. Lincoln, martyred in his moment of triumph, kept the nation intact through the travail of civil war. The American people will always be in his debt. But why Jefferson?

The third in a line of forty-three presidents, he left office having alienated an entire section of the country. He missed the Constitutional Convention while serving as minister to France during the summer of 1787, so he is not strictly speaking a Founding Father. Even his authoring the Declaration of Independence is a somewhat exaggerated claim to greatness, for the document was actually the report of a committee for which Jefferson acted as penman. Moreover, ever since Southern Secession, his two constitutional positions have carried some blame for plunging the nation into a fratricidal war just thirty-five years after his death.

The conventional explanation for his monument is that Jefferson embodied the spirit of the Enlightenment, which itself was made tangible in a nation conceived in liberty and dedicated to the proposition that all men are created equal. Here the range of Jefferson's sympathies is called into play—his dedication as a student of nature, his talents as an

This chapter first appeared as "Without Resolution: The Jeffersonian Tension in American Nationalism," Harmsworth Inaugural Lecture, April 25, 1991, and is reprinted by permission of Oxford University Press.

19

amateur anthropologist, his craft as an architect, his philanthropy in education, and his accomplishments as a reformer. The one revolutionary leader who remains to this day a freshet of wise observations, Jefferson also inspires affection as the perdurable optimist, the practical dreamer, and the well-tempered statesman. But is it enough to merit one of three presidential monuments?

Jefferson's detractors would answer my question by calling attention to the way he engrossed admirers by speaking on both sides of every issue. "Which Thomas Jefferson do you quote?" runs the title of a querulous article about the sage of Monticello.[1] It's an interesting query. The militant Populists of the late nineteenth century cherished him as the protector of an endangered agrarian way of life while Roosevelt's New Dealers hailed him as the champion of scientific agriculture. Nationalists remember him for organizing the country's first political party and purchasing Louisiana, events conveniently forgotten by those who credit him with the doctrine of states' rights and the strict construction of the Constitution. Even more indicative of his utility to both sides of every argument is the fact that antislavery activists and slavery defenders alike count him as one of their own. He wrote slavery out of the Northwest Territories but passionately supported its extension into the first new state carved from the Louisiana Purchase, his so-called Empire of Liberty. Jefferson, moreover, has the unique distinction of being claimed as the founder of both major American political parties.

The answer to my question speaks to Jefferson's role or, more precisely, his implication in the central tensions in Americans' self-understanding. Jefferson, more than any other leader, had a vision of what America should stand for. The phrase itself suggests the problem. The United States in 1776 had to stand for something because the states did not possess any other cohering force. Unlike the other kingdoms and commonwealths of the eighteenth century, they had no common history, no shared understanding of social authority or divine intentions. The regions that composed the United States—New England, the mid-Atlantic area, and the South—had their own traditions, but these excluded outsiders and hence stood in the way of an integrative identity for the whole. Other countries mindlessly acquired solidarity by living over time in the same place, but Americans were strangers, if not actually invaders, in the land they occupied. They could draw no spiritual sustenance from having lived long in the land, and they had purposefully rooted out the one unifying force in their corporate lives—the sovereign presence of British rule.

Lacking the resonating symbols of shared experience that Edmund Burke evoked for England, Americans had to self-consciously construct them. Political institutions alone joined the diverse states, so it is not surprising that the themes for a collective identity coalesced during presidential elections. Jefferson was the first person to challenge an incumbent president, and the campaign he waged turned on the meaning to be given to the American Revolution. In winning in 1800 he secured the presidency for his party for three decades, long enough to determine that the United States would not just be; it would stand for something. Its coherence would come from beliefs, from statements of high principles and abiding truths, from a creed that spoke of liberty and equality, natural rights and human nature. Far from Jefferson's contradictory positions being flaws in an otherwise clearheaded thinker, they constitute his enduring appeal, for he was both the author and the mediator of the central tensions in American nationalism.

The prevailing concept of ideology can illuminate my point. In ideology scholars have found a concept that enables them to talk about thinking as a social activity. Ideologies are not formal intellectual systems that discipline the mind but loose associations of ideas that engage the emotions. Ideologies generate enthusiasms, commitments, and prejudices. They provide us with the means for expressing our religion, our science, our laws, and our fantasies. Ideologies minister to the individual's need to comprehend the world as a meaningful whole and to society's need for implicit understandings among its members. More than mere communication systems, ideologies promote agreement and inspire action. They define roles, project fears, fashion programs, create identities, direct attention, and supply transcendent meaning. Availing myself of the distinction between the intellectual and the ideological, I would say that Jefferson's great contribution was not intellectual—not the creation of a coherent and logical philosophy—but ideological—the fusing of emotionally charged convictions into a single discursive grid.

A man who might have perished as an American academic, Jefferson wrote just one book, *Notes on the State of Virginia*. But during his life span of eighty-three years, he composed several hundred official reports, eight presidential addresses, an autobiographical fragment, and more than 18,000 letters, the bulk of them carefully noted in his Summary Journal, a 656-page register and index of his correspondence from 1783 to 1826.[2] In the bicentenary year of his birth in 1943, Princeton University committed itself to bringing out a modern edition of his complete papers. Funded by the *New York Times*, this project soon became the model for the great documentary publishing enterprises of the post–World War II era. Forty-eight years later, the twenty-second volume was published covering Jefferson's papers through his service as secretary of state under Washington. Ahead lie the years as opposition leader, vice president, presidential candidate, two-term president, state reform leader, and founder of the University of Virginia. The projected completion date for this editorial enterprise is 2050—which will be the centenary of volume 1 of the Jefferson Papers.

One thinks of Jefferson in relation to the people he wrote—Jefferson and John Adams—the American versions of the archetypal Roundhead and Cavalier; Jefferson and James Madison, the great Virginia collaborators, the one founder of America's first political party and the other, father of the U.S. Constitution; Jefferson and Pierre Samuel Du Pont de Nemours, the philosophers of the New and Old Worlds; Jefferson and Joseph Priestley, Jefferson and Maria Cosway, Jefferson and Abigail Adams. This pairing of Jefferson with others is the result of his coming to us through his correspondence, but it also characterizes his being in the world—animated by compelling interests, mobilized by his desire to persuade others, attended to because of his capacity to frame moral ambitions in evocative prose.

Nowhere is this more in evidence than in the Declaration of Independence, which sets forth the causes that impelled the colonies to dissolve their political ties to Great Britain. One can render it conversationally: "We hold these truth to be self-evident, that all men are created equal, that they are endowed by their Creator with certain unalienable rights, that among these are life, liberty, and the pursuit of happiness. That to secure these rights, governments are instituted among men, deriving their just powers from the consent of the governed." Implicit in these simple affirmations are the kinds of rights being simultaneously disavowed—those connected to the English tradition—specific, concrete, and traceable to particular historic events. The rights of Englishmen had failed the American colonists so they migrated intellectually toward an abstract, rationalist theory of rights.

The Declaration did not break new ground in political philosophy. Its conceptual roots were firmly planted in the soil of seventeenth-century England, and many who signed it saw no conflict between natural rights and their adherence to a traditional social order. The radical potential of the Declaration only revealed itself in the ensuing twenty-five years and then principally because of Jefferson's exertions to prevent a restrictive interpretation of the principles of 1776. It was Jefferson who spoke to the aspirations of ordinary Americans in that critical quarter century when a national identity was being formed and he who promoted a literal reading of such phrases as natural equality and popular sovereignty.

The great obstruction to our view of the past is the period lying between our own time and the one we seek to know, for in those years events are taken in, as it were, grasped, described, narrated, and analyzed. In this process we fold the details of the known into our understanding of reality in general, sealing off our imagination from alternative explanations. Nothing is more difficult to see in the past than that which has subsequently become familiar. What actually happened in retrospect is perceived not only as probable but often as inevitable. To say, for instance, that Thomas Jefferson built a political party around the proposition that all men are created equal and endowed with inalienable rights seems bland if not outright banal. To say further that he worked feverishly for eight years to stir his countrymen to protect their liberty, strike down privilege, limit government, and extend the ambit of free choice is to imagine Jefferson pushing hard on an open door.

When Jefferson took his case to an electorate unused to partisan politics—the year would have been 1793—the positions of power in the newly constituted United States were held by men who were socially conservative and intellectually unadventurous. Many, including Vice President Adams, drew their truths from a kind of secular Calvinism, an amalgam of wisdom drawn from the classics and the Bible. Men are prone to sin and society subject to degenerative diseases, they stressed. The novelty of the United States lay not in signaling a new dispensation for the human race, but in offering learned statesmen an opportunity to apply the lessons of the past. According to these national leaders, when the American colonies separated from Great Britain, they freed themselves from the Mother Country's corruptions, but not from the pure model itself, which taught that order preceded freedom and that gentlemen filtered from the mass of the voters through elaborate electoral processes could alone preserve that order.

These were the political views that the Jeffersonians attacked. Going behind Federalist policies, they exposed the social premises on which they were based. Taking advantage of a male literacy rate near 90 percent and a reading public addicted to newspapers, they developed a flourishing opposition press, too flourishing for the Federalists who after five years of partisan invective passed a draconian sedition law. Prosecutions shut down every Jeffersonian newspaper in the country. In Philadelphia, the capital city, former comrades in arms crossed the street rather than acknowledge each other's presence with the courtesy of a raised hat.

Appalled by the government's sedition prosecutions, Jefferson, who had become vice president when Adams was elected president, sought the security of Monticello to draft resolutions calling on the states to reject the federal law. Passions were running so high that Jefferson actually believed that army maneuvers on the northern border of Virginia were meant to intimidate him. Two fully formed parties faced each other in 1800, both convinced that the election was about securing the revolution. Jefferson won and took office at the head of a political movement that had turned the rationale for independence into a manifesto for government opposed to all social distinctions. The campaign had produced such bitterness that his old friend Adams departed for Massachusetts before the inauguration, leaving behind a curt message saying that the seven horses, two carriages, and harnesses at the White House were property of the U.S. government. Not given to vainglorious remarks, Jefferson hailed his victory as a second American Revolution: "as real a revolution in the principles of our government as that of 1776 was in its form."[3]

The Jeffersonian tension alluded to in the chapter title emerged from the ideas that he popularized in his campaign for president and acted on during his eight years in the White House. The most obvious contradiction in the foundation of the United States was the presence of slavery in a nation that dedicated itself to individual liberty. The manifest hypocrisy of slavery in a free society prompted the first emancipation movement, as each northern state passed legislation outlawing future slavery. Here the battle could be framed as an antagonism between an ancient institution and an enlightened zeal for liberation from the mores of "dark and slavish times." The old was indicted by the new with the United States fulfilling its mission to break paths and bear torches. It is a testament to the unthinking subordination of women that only the contradiction between the Declaration and slavery abraded consciences.

The tension that I have in mind, however, is something less obvious and comes from the way that Jefferson's natural rights doctrine generated new prejudices that raised hidden obstacles not only to the work of southern emancipation but also to the extension of rights to freed slaves and aliens. A further tension emerged from the Jeffersonian assumption that economic and political freedom were mutually supporting. In his success as president and party leader Jefferson sowed the seeds for two enduring conflicts in American life: the first issuing from the rooting of natural rights in a theory about invariant human nature and the second from the expectation of the natural compatibility of equality and liberty. These tensions are characterized in the chapter title as "without resolution." To understand why this is so we must look to their author.

The source of Jefferson's radical enthusiasms is indeed a mystery. He was not an outsider; he was not a dissenter; he was not a rebel (except perhaps in the eyes of George III). Rather he grew up and remained within the established gentry of Virginia. On his mother's side Jefferson was connected to several mighty tidewater families and thus he was born into the dense cousinry that ruled Virginia. At his father's early death he inherited a 7,000-acre plantation and 180 slaves. Admitted to the bar at age twenty-three, Jefferson lived the life of a country lawyer while mastering the subjects that furnished his capacious mind: law, political theory, history, geology, natural philosophy, architecture, and linguistics. Like many other American leaders, he won fame first as the author of a revolutionary pamphlet, *Summary View of the Rights of British America* (1774). Sent by Virginia to the Second Continental Congress, Jefferson took up his seat just as news of the battle of Bunker Hill reached Philadelphia. After a year of agonizing indecision, Congress voted to declare independence in 1776 and Jefferson was chosen to join the declaration-drafting committee because of his "peculiar felicity of expression." Following his wartime service as governor of Virginia and member of Congress he became minister to France in 1784 where, as he graciously commented, he succeeded Benjamin Franklin because no one could replace him.

James Duane, a New York leader, described Jefferson as the best rubber-off of dust he had ever met.[4] The metaphor is apt because it was Jefferson's peculiar relation to the settled and stationary—those things that collect dust—that separated him from almost all of his peers in the revolutionary elite. The natural rights philosophy did not represent for him, as it did for others, an intellectual discourse going back to the Stoics. Rather it announced a new, liberating program directed to dismantling the old social order so that men, so long alienated from their true natures, might recover them. For Jefferson, like Thomas Paine, the implementation of natural rights required radical surgery on the traditional body politic. More urgently, the dead hand of the past had to be lifted from the shoulders of the living. But, unlike Paine, Jefferson was no deracinated intellectual; he plotted his reform campaign within the bosom of America's triumphant revolutionary elite.

During his years as American minister in Paris Jefferson became fascinated with the idea of replacing the tacit consent of the governed with a genuine, explicit endorsement of current laws. "The earth belongs in usufruct to the living," he wrote Madison.[5] Then taking the proposition quite literally, he set about calculating the optimal space of years between appeals to the electorate if each generation were to hold its own plebiscite on the body of legislation ruling their lives. Jefferson saw the past's restrictive force in language also. If existing laws constrained each cohort of the living, how much more profoundly inhibiting was the conceptual vocabulary one inherited through language. Jefferson targeted the purist as the enemy of linguistic freedom. Dilating on two words he had just learned, purism and neologism, he announced, "I am not a friend to what is called purism, but a jealous one to the neology which has introduced these two new words into our dictionary without any authority. I consider purism as destroying the verve and beauty of the language while neology improves both and adds to its copiousness."[6]

Jefferson defined dictionaries as the repositories of words already legitimated by usage. Resorting to the metaphor of production, he called society the workshop for words. The principal neologisms of his own day were the "isms." The *Oxford English Dictionary* (OED) credits

Jefferson with coining the word "Americanism," when he borrowed it from a Scottish clergyman, John Witherspoon. But he accepted the new conceptual universe the "isms" reflected—a world where shared conviction could create political affinities as easily as economic interests or inherited allegiances. Liberalism too he claimed, although the words "capitalism" and "individualism," the reality for which he helped shape, come from the verbal inventiveness of the next generation. Warming to the subject of language, Jefferson further noted (and I hesitate to share his thoughts with readers) "that if in the process of sound neologization our transatlantic brethren do not choose to accompany us we may furnish after the Ionian a second example of a colonial dialect improving on its primitive."[7]

Jefferson's receptivity to neology, neologisms, and neologization was not shared by his friend John Adams, with whom he resumed a correspondence in old age. "Pray explain to me this Neological Title!" Adams wrote Jefferson in reference to a book about ideology. "What does it Mean? When Bonaparte used it I was delighted with it, upon the Common Principle of delight in every Thing we cannot understand. Does it mean Idiotism? The Science of Non Compos Menticism. The Science of Lunacy. The Theory of Delerium. Or does it mean the Science of Self Love? of Amour Propre?"[8] Thus Adams gently ribbed his friend's unflagging love of the new.

A brilliant wordsmith, Jefferson used metaphors like levers thrust against the settled opinions of his peers. When in 1786 an armed band of indebted farmers in western Massachusetts closed the county courts to prevent foreclosure proceedings, they frightened no less a cool head than George Washington. Jefferson, who heard the news in Paris, put a different construction on the events. He reminded his correspondents that the thirteen American states had been independent for eleven years and then—giving early proof of what can be done with statistics—he calculated that this amounted to 143 years of political life for the nation as a whole. "What country before ever existed a century and a half without a rebellion?" he asked rhetorically. "What signify a few lives lost in a century or two? The tree of liberty must be refreshed from time to time with the blood of patriots and tyrants. It is its natural manure." Sensing on another occasion an effort to elevate the new U.S. Constitution into a national shrine, Jefferson ridiculed those who looked on constitutions with "sanctimonious reverence and deemed them like the Ark of the Covenant too sacred to be touched."[9]

Even more extravagantly libertarian was his defense of the Jacobins in early 1793. Responding to the dismayed reports of an American eyewitness in Paris, Jefferson reminded him that "the liberty of the whole earth was depending on the issue of the contest . . . rather that it should have failed, I would have seen half the earth desolated. Were there but an Adam and an Eve left in every country, and left free, it would be better than as it now is."[10] Eve's presence here in fact was gratuitous, for Jefferson never extended his liberating zeal to women. In his view they were disqualified by nature to participate in politics. But surely few practical men, entrusted repeatedly by their peers with positions of responsibility, have seriously entertained as many subversive ideas as Thomas Jefferson.

The past for Jefferson contained frozen privileges and moribund arrangements. The reigning ideas of old regime societies were embodied in forms that impressed themselves in the rituals, ceremonies, and decorum of everyday life. People lived, as it were, in a masque cut off from their real selves as they performed the parts imposed by the hierarchical institutions of church and state. For Jefferson ideas were meant to liberate rather than prescribe. In countries "left free" the forms of social existence would be emergent and fluid. Without set practices, enduring laws, reverenced constitutions, and confining vocabularies, experience itself would furnish the mind with the material for making decisions. Liberated once and for all would be man the doer, the inventor, the adapter, the improver—Homo faber—the universal man hidden from himself by tyrants, priests, and overlords. "We can no longer say there is nothing new under the sun," Jefferson wrote Priestley shortly after his election to president. "For this whole chapter in the history of man is new. The great extent of our Republic is new. Its sparse habitation is new. The mighty wave of public opinion which has rolled over it is new."[11]

Jefferson's virulent Anglophobia also fed on his contempt for the veneration of the past, which he read into English pride in their constitution. He had, however, left hostages in his lifelong vendetta against Great Britain in the form of his intellectual heroes—Bacon, Locke, and Newton. Some might consider their greatness as casting glory on the nation that produced them, but Jefferson found a graphic way to separate his philosophical fathers from their English heritage. He commissioned three drawings of the men arranged in the same oval frame. Because they were "the founders of the physical and moral sciences" they should not be confounded "with the herd of other great men," he wrote a friend, adding that they were "the three greatest men that had ever lived, without any exception."[12] Thus detached, Bacon, Newton, and Locke became universal heroes. Like the rights of men, these creative geniuses were associated with nature, not history.

Both Europeans and Americans contributed to the symbolic construction of the new nation, what one scholar has called the "mirage in the West." Enlightenment pamphleteers had put a radical spin on the doctrine of original sin. Demoted, it was recast as ignorance or wrongheadedness, but American innocence was more specific yet. "The characteristic difference between your revolution and ours," Madame d'Houdetot wrote to Jefferson,

> is that having nothing to destroy, you had nothing to injure, and labouring for a people, few in number, incorrupted, and extended over a large tract of country, you have avoided all the inconvenience of a situation, contrary in every respect. Every step in your revolution was perhaps the effect of virtue, while ours are often faults, and sometimes crimes.[13]

Americans had escaped contamination from the past; they had been prized free of the original sin that was Europe, washing it away in a transatlantic crossing. A conceptual blind had been lowered over the violence of slavery and conquest that was indigenous to the United States.

Accepting the challenge of interpreting natural design, Jefferson turned himself into an agent of change—profound, transformative change in the social relations and political forms of his nation. The course of American politics was not set by the War for Independence, nor the ratification of the Constitution. To steer into uncharted waters required a new tack and a new helmsman, and Jefferson provided both. However stereotypical his Enlightenment faith in revolutionary change might have been, his opportunity to act on his ideas as the leader of a political movement that carried him to the presidency of his country was unique.

For him the battle was a straightforward engagement between clarity and darkness, between the party of principled men and the party of rogues that he said typified political divisions. But he could not have appreciated the ideological dimensions of his enterprise. From the distance of two hundred years we can observe which intellectual connections had become uncoupled in Jefferson's day and which ideas lay waiting to be fused into a new configuration of belief.

The dethroning of the past and the diminishing of public authority, which Jefferson both reflected and hurried along, were made possible by the unraveling of Christian unity in America. Earlier, the Protestants' longing to partake of God's perfection had led them to inhabit a world of elaborate linkages that joined their lives to the sacred drama of a predestined universe. Church and communicant partook of a divine order that alone gave meaning to human existence. But in the latter part of the eighteenth century, material ambitions and sectarian rivalry chipped away at that core concept of a common fate. By the century's end, America's churches, like its male citizens, had been individualized and endowed with rights to life, liberty, and the pursuit of private truths. Paradoxically, a skeptic like Jefferson attracted many Christians because his championship of personal liberty protected them from the intolerant zeal of other Christians.

The United States in 1800 was poised on the eve of a great evangelical movement, but this successful repietizing of American society did not strengthen religious institutions. It spoke to the solitary sinner rather than the corporate Christian enterprise, leaving the converted as islands of holiness, cut off from the cohering force of a dominant church. Like Jeffersonian liberalism, American Protestantism rejected the past, indifferent alike to the historic church and its traditions. The individual, not the congregation, became the locus of religious power in America. The proliferation of denominations advertised the freedom of religion even as it necessitated the wall of separation between church and state that Jefferson erected verbally.

Meanwhile nature had come to dominate the social imagination of the Jeffersonians—the nature that Bacon, Newton, and Locke had made orderly, comprehensive, and knowable. Beneath the myriad of surface variety and detail, the natural philosophers had discovered regularities and uniformities of lawlike certainty. The pulling apart of Christian corporatism opened the possibility of finding unity in nature and what Jefferson called "nature's God." Nature provided authority as well. Scientific investigators exuded a mastery over causes with their discovery of patterns and processes, even as they referred the responsibility for effects to natural design.

Categorized by specialists and analyzed under the ruling principle of function, nature offered a new context for understanding human institutions. However, to detach society from the domain of politics and study it as a manifestation of nature was to alter dramatically the character of social inquiry. No less discriminatory of bad and good than the sacred order it replaced, the natural order assigned moral worth to those human arrangements that conformed to the objective and irresistible laws of cause and effect. "What is" became the insistent question, replacing "what ought to be." These inferences from the new sciences, familiar to all students of the Enlightenment, had a special conceptual career in the United States where they became fundamental axioms of an emergent ideology. What could only be entertained as theory in Europe could be accepted by sensible Americans as a description of how things actually were. Moreover, throwing a searchlight upon nature as the author of America's liberal forms simultaneously cast into the shadows their social construction.

By construing liberty as liberation from historic institutions, Jefferson made America the pilot society for the world. It was not Americans but all men who sought freedom from past oppression. While the world may have been indifferent to these claims, for Americans the presumed universality of their values turned them into empirical propositions about human nature. The assertion that all men are alike in their aspirations to freedom as well as their capacity to pursue independent lives provided the scientific underpinnings to America's national creed. It also relieved Americans from the burden of history that links one generation to another through inherited responsibilities. With reality as the dispenser of rewards and punishments, a different kind of freedom could be conceived, one that consisted of subordination to nature alone.

A philosophy that taught that nature disclosed the moral ends of human life and then read nature as endowing each man with a right to pursue his own happiness comported well with the actual biases of most Americans, but it created what I call a Jeffersonian tension with its confounding of facts and ideals. America's natural rights philosophy did not just express aspirations; it purported to explain reality. Its assertions were both normative and prescriptive. Factually, it taught that all men are the same; philosophically, that all men should have equal rights; but practically only those men who met the liberty-loving, self-improving ideal were freely admitted to the category "all men." Over time, the language of uniformity turned differences into deviations. Discursively those people who strayed from the established norm became deviants. And if they were denied their rights, it was nature that authored the exception. We can see these assumptions operating most powerfully and most conspicuously in relation to Africans and Indians.

The actual architects of American slavery—the seventeenth-century colonists who passed the laws that specified who and what a slave was—used racial difference as an implement of control. It was not just a case of making Africans the subjects of enslavement, but more insidiously of changing slavery from a juridical status to a racial category. Race became the defining feature of Anglo-American slavery and over the years its social consequences were attributed to the genetic inheritance of a particular people, the nurture of enslavement merging imperceptibly with the nature of the enslaved.

This deliberate confounding of nature and nurture—common enough in human experience—assumed portentous importance when the idea of a uniform human nature was linked to the right to life, liberty, and the pursuit of happiness. It is against this philosophical background that Jefferson's remarks in the *Notes on the State of Virginia* should be weighed. There Jefferson expressed what he called a suspicion that Negroes were inferior to the whites in the endowments both of body and mind. It was not their condition but nature that had made blacks inferior to whites.[14]

Jefferson, the slaveholder, was implicated in all the system's evils, including its rationalizations. He inherited, bought, and acquired from his wife over two hundred slaves on whom he relied for plantation labor and domestic service. Throughout his life he sold slaves to offset debts, thus participating in the cruelest aspect of slavery. When his slaves ran away, as they did frequently, he hired slave catchers to bring them back. His farm book, as carefully kept as one would expect from the meticulous Jefferson, records the punishments meted out to runaways, penned in his own fine script.

Nor did Jefferson escape contamination from the endemic sexual exploitation of black women. Some believe that he fathered four children with his slave, Sally Hemings. The extant, largely circumstantial evidence can neither prove nor disprove this charge. Not debatable at all, however, is the parentage of Sally Hemings and her three siblings who came to Jefferson from his wife's estate and were the offspring of his father-in-law, John Wayles. Hence, Jefferson's slave force contained the half-sisters and brothers of his wife. Here was the material for a Greek tragedy. And the enormity of slavery occasionally broke Jefferson's composure. "I tremble for my country when I reflect that God is just, and that his justice cannot sleep forever," he wrote a friend while in his *Notes on the State of Virginia* he detailed the psychological bonds that froze the participants of slavery into permanent enmity: "The whole commerce between master and slave is a perpetual exercise of the most boisterous passions, the most unremitting despotism on the one part, and degrading submission on the other. . . . The man must be a prodigy who can retain his manners and morals undepraved by such circumstances."[15]

A declared enemy of slavery, Jefferson moved against the South's peculiar institution with caution. He formulated the exclusion that kept slavery out of the Northwest Territory, but acquiesced in the spread of slavery into the Southwest. As a reviser of Virginia's colonial laws, he proposed a scheme for gradual emancipation but withdrew it from consideration at the last moment. And most importantly his emancipation proposals always contained the provision that freed blacks be carried out of the state and colonized elsewhere. He could tolerate the races living together in slavery; he could not envision a biracial society of freed men and women. He made his reservations explicit:

> Deep-rooted prejudices entertained by the whites, ten thousand recollections, by the blacks, of the injuries they have sustained, new provocations, the real distinctions which nature has made; and many other circumstances will divide us into parties and produce convulsions, which will probably never end but in the extermination of one or the other race.[16]

Native Americans were similarly caught in the Jeffersonian tension. For them it was not innate inferiority but cultural obstinacy that accounted for their disqualifying differences. Jefferson evinced much more sympathy for Native Americans than for Africans. Fascinated by language, he collected Indian vocabularies. Despite his anthropological curiosity about Native American culture, he favored the amalgamation of the Indians into white American society. As president he first pursued an assimilationist policy. "Explain to the native chiefs," he wrote the territorial governor, "that they must give up the communal chase and take up farming. Tell them that they can then bring their women in from the fields."[17] When the Indians showed little enthusiasm for this project, Jefferson reversed his position and adopted a policy of Indian removal. He reverted to a position that he had earlier confided to the revolutionary commander George Rogers Clark: "If we are to wage a campaign against these Indians the end proposed should be their extermination, or their removal beyond the lakes of the Illinois river. The same world will scarcely do for them and us."[18] As with the Afro-Americans, the differences of the Indians—their willed preference to retain their native ways—eliminated them from the grand human destiny that the American nation had come to embody. It was a grim testimony to Jefferson's commitment to uniformity. Indian culture, black memory—both served to exclude Indians and Africans from the liberating potential of American institutions even as those institutions continued to claim universal applicability. In another generation, the distinguishing marks of immigrant culture ran athwart the liberal thrust of American social theory with its naturalizing and systematizing of human experience.

The master passion of Jefferson's revolutionary generation was not, however, to build a multiracial society but rather to erect republics for white men.[19] To do this, Jefferson gave expression to one of the most attractive propositions of the American experiment: that political and economic liberty could eradicate the differences imposed by ignorance, superstition, and tyranny. Working together, economic and political liberty would serve each other's moral purposes as they reformed a world distorted by accumulated abuses of the past. Access to economic opportunity and political participation would strip away artificial barriers, leaving men as men to prosper in a new era of equality of esteem. This animating hope of American liberalism secured the loyalty of the poor to economic liberty and the patronage of the rich for political liberty.

Looking back on his legislative record, Jefferson claimed to have created a system "by which every fibre would be eradicated of antient or future aristocracy." At death's door he reiterated his great hope: "The general spread of the light of science has already laid open to every view the palpable truth, that the mass of mankind has not been born with saddles on their backs, nor a favored few booted and spurred, ready to ride them legitimately." Jefferson explicitly detached liberty from its Spartan connection to the discipline of denial and reattached it to the promise of prosperity. His optimism floated on expectations of material abundance. His goals required material means. Too much land, he believed, fostered the savage condition, but without land men could not achieve personal autonomy. His draft constitution for Virginia included a fifty-acre property qualification for voting, but simultaneously he proposed giving all landless adult white men fifty acres. Spurning Malthus's gloomy predictions, he insisted that in America, harvests grew exponentially. The opportunity for productive efforts enabled him to square the circle of self-interest and community welfare. "So invariably do the laws of nature create our duties and interests," he wrote the French economist J. B. Say, "that when they seem to be at variance, we ought to suspect some fallacy in our reasoning."[20]

In Jefferson's famous line that "all men are created equal and endowed by their Creator with certain unalienable rights" equality is made to lie down with liberty much like the lamb with the lion. In the same sentence egalitarianism and liberalism have unreflectively been joined. Like the conflict between abstract universals and particular deviations, the tension between equality and liberty remains obscured by a national ideology that asserts their compatibility. Indeed the fit between equality and liberty is so intuitively satisfying that Americans have had great difficulty confronting the built-in tendency for free enterprise to promote concentrations of wealth and, with them, concentrations of power. More like a competitive sport than the exemplification of natural justice, the exercise of personal liberty in a persistently buoyant economy has produced winners and losers, while narrowing the life chances for many and turning economic and political liberty into increasingly formal propositions.

Despite his conviction that the earth belongs to the living, Jefferson recoiled from the proposition to curtail inheritance:

> To take from one because it is thought his own industry and that of his father had acquired too much in order to spare to others who, or whose fathers have not exercised equal industry and skill, is to violate arbitrarily the first principle of association, the guarantee to everyone a free exercise of his industry and the fruits acquired by it.[21]

The simplicity of this expression would lead one to think that Jefferson could not conceive of concentrated wealth being passed from one generation to another were it not for his knowledge that the wealth of one race had perpetuated the enslavement of another.

The tension that remains unresolved in American nationalism centers on the issue of otherness. Attacking the complex forms of old regime social distinctions, Americans gave a peculiarly powerful meaning to natural rights by insisting on the real and fundamental sameness of human nature. This assertion formed the bedrock of the American creed—simultaneously serving as a scientific proposition and a moral claim—against which evidence of diversity could only provoke intense anxiety. The idea of representing universal human nature elevated the American nation, but in this elevation was hidden a hostility to differences whether created by genetic endowments, social customs, or economic outcomes. Lofty as the sonorous phrases of the Declaration of Independence are, they should be read for the variety they deny as well as the sameness they affirm. Because the distinctions of the Old World were so often invidious, most Americans could celebrate their rejection. Yet more than privilege was abandoned. To tolerate human differences is to acknowledge the residual consequences of past living, to accept the fact that we enter the drama of life in the middle of the act. The Jeffersonians wiped clean the slate by looking beyond the abundant diversity of their society to the presumed uniformity of human nature. The claim of lawlike consistency endowed the doctrine of natural rights with its special force. To abandon the literal assertion of a uniform human nature was to leave natural rights exposed as mere goals; to retain it was to provide scientific validation to America's unique political forms.

It would be a grave error of historical judgment to underestimate the significance of Jefferson's crusade against the tyrannies of the past. Only an absence of familiarity would lead us to believe that the hidden injuries of class were more damaging than the conspicuous abuses of status. Nor is it the case that traditional societies do not have their outsiders, their ostracized men and women pushed to the margins of collective life. Their biases, however, are usually justified as protecting tradition whereas liberalism proclaims a universal fellowship and then leaves nature to determine its membership.

The Jeffersonian idiom still structures the discourse of rights. If we are to extend their range and penetration in our own time, we will need to disentangle them from those eighteenth-century propositions that standardized human ambition. Perhaps we should acknowledge as well that rights are based on a love of justice that is nurtured by society, not laws arising from the study of nature.

There is a deep human longing for a fresh start—an empty canvas, a blank slate, a present washed clean of the failed performances of the past. Believing in a fresh start rather than merely longing for one required a new explanation of the human situation. Jefferson offered one in his exalting the influence of nature over history, and he grafted the promise of that fresh start onto the tree of liberty. The fruit has been a succession of new starts for America—Theodore Roosevelt's New Nationalism and Franklin Roosevelt's New Deal, Wilson's New Freedom, Kennedy's New Frontier, Reagan's New Federalism. From the "New Order for the Ages" emblazoned on the Great Seal of the Republic in 1782 to George Bush's New World Order two centuries later, Americans have sought to reexperience the liberating act of their revolution.

Accepting this invitation to newness has entailed rejecting the past with its historic memory and cultural particulars cluttering the social landscape. For America's revolutionary generation, Indian removal and African colonization symbolically and actually tied Jefferson's vision of liberty to the elimination of diversity. The new dispensation for mankind was to be written across an empty continent. The tension in American ideology has remained taut throughout the history of the United States and Jefferson has made it bearable. On his authority Americans have been able to sustain rather than abandon the inherent conflicts in their affirmation of universal freedom and their intolerance of social diversity.

Frequently exposing himself and his ideological heirs to charges of bad faith, Jefferson found unresolved tensions a lesser evil than despair.

When Adams and Jefferson began writing again after their retirement from public office, they tactfully explored the foundations of their opposing views. Adams was characteristically crusty, using his words to jab and thrust at the stupidities of the world while Jefferson calmly steered his philosophical ship into untroubled waters. Like his native New England, Adams held a view of human nature that owed more to John Calvin than John Locke. One wonders if Jefferson caught the irony when Adams commented, "Your taste is judicious in liking better the dreams of the Future, than the History of the Past." Their thirteen-year correspondence was ended by death, which amazingly came to both men on July 4, 1826, the fiftieth anniversary of the Declaration of Independence that they had helped write. On his deathbed, Adams's thoughts turned to his old friend and political rival. His last words were: "Thomas Jefferson still survives." So too do Thomas Jefferson's ideals and the tensions they generated.[22]

NOTES

1. Clinton Rossiter, "Which Thomas Jefferson Do You Quote?" *Reporter* 17 (September 15, 1955).

2. John Catanzariti, "Thomas Jefferson: Correspondent" (unpublished paper, 1989).

3. Jefferson to Spencer Roane, September 6, 1819, in *The Writings of Thomas Jefferson*, ed. Paul L. Ford (New York, 1892–99), x, 140.

4. I have learned that it was James Duane, not William Duane, the fiery Irish journalist, who made this remark about Jefferson.

5. Jefferson to Madison, September 6, 1789, in *The Papers of Thomas Jefferson*, ed. Julian P. Boyd et al. (Princeton, 1950–), xv, 392–97.

6. *The Living Thoughts of Thomas Jefferson*, ed. John Dewey (London, 1941), 9.

7. Dewey, ed., *Living Thoughts of Thomas Jefferson*, 9.

8. Adams to Jefferson, December 16, 1816, in *The Adams-Jefferson Letters: The Complete Correspondence Between Thomas Jefferson and Abigail and John Adams*, ed. Lester J. Cappon (Chapel Hill, N.C., 1959), ii, 500–501.

9. Jefferson to William Stephens Smith, November 13, 1787, in Boyd et al., *Papers of Jefferson*, xii, 355–56; Jefferson to Samuel Kercheval, July 12, 1816, in Ford, *Writings of Jefferson*, x, 42.

10. Jefferson to William Short, January 3, 1793, in *The Life and Writings of Thomas Jefferson*, ed. Adrienne Koch and William Peden (New York, 1944), 321–22.

11. Jefferson to Priestley, March 21, 1801, in Ford, *Writings of Jefferson*, vii, 54–56.

12. Jefferson to John Trumbull, February 15, 1789, in Boyd et al., *Papers of Thomas Jefferson*, 14:561.

13. Madame d'Houdetot to Jefferson, September 3, 1790, as quoted in *Les Amities Americaines de Madame d'Houdetot, d'apres sa correspondance inedite avec Benjamin Franklin et Thomas Jefferson*, ed. Gilbert Chinard (Paris, 1924), 56.

14. William Cohen, "Thomas Jefferson and the Problem of Slavery," *Journal of American History* 56 (1969).

15. DNA tests have shown that a male Jefferson fathered Sally Hemings's son Eston. While there were eighteen men with Jefferson's genetic inheritance living at the time, only Jefferson shared a living space with Hemings. "The Jefferson Scandal," in *Fame and the Founding Fathers: Essays by Douglass Adair*, ed. Trevor Colbourn (New York, 1974); Merrill D. Peterson, *Thomas Jefferson and the New Nation: A Biography* (New York, 1970), 260–61; *Notes on the State of Virginia*, ed. William Peden (Chapel Hill, N.C., 1955), 161.

16. Peden, *Notes on the State of Virginia*, 138.

17. Bernard W. Sheehan, *Seeds of Extinction: Jeffersonian Philanthropy and the American Indian* (Chapel Hill, N.C., 1973), 168–81, 244–50.

18. Jefferson to George Rogers Clark, January 1, 1780, in Boyd et al., *Jefferson Papers*, iii, 259.

19. I am indebted to William Freehling for this line. See "Slavery and the Founding Fathers," *American Historical Review* 77 (1972).

20. Boyd et al., *Papers of Jefferson*, ii, 308; Jefferson to J. B. Say, February 1, 1804, in *The Writings of Thomas Jefferson*, ed. A. A. Lipscomb and A. A. Bergh (Washington, D.C., 1903), xi, 2–3.

21. Jefferson to Joseph Milligan, April 6, 1816, in Lipscomb and Bergh, *Writings of Thomas Jefferson*, xiv, 466. He favored taxation explicitly designed to reduce inequalities in wealth.

22. Adams to Jefferson, August 9, 1816, in Cappon, *Adams-Jefferson Letters*, ii, 487.

2

A DIFFERENT KIND OF INDEPENDENCE: THE POSTWAR RESTRUCTURING OF THE HISTORICAL STUDY OF EARLY AMERICA

For Americans, writing and teaching the history of their own country represents a special intellectual enterprise, different from that of studying Germany or China or Nigeria. Like all histories, national history springs from the human fascination with self-discovery, from persistent concerns about the nature of social existence and our engagement with it. But with American history, a relatively open-ended search about the past collides with the vigilant censors of patriotic pride and national self-imaging. Through the years, these censors have been most invested in the proposition that the United States marks out the political path of the future, leaving historians to scour the past for evidence of this role. Since American progress had first become manifest with the nation-building acts of revolution and constitution writing, the seventeenth and eighteenth centuries were turned into a prologue to the history of the United States, the pathbreaking republic and exemplary society. Declaring their independence from this Whiggish historiography, early American historians of the last generation have attached themselves to a European frame of reference that, perversely, has had a liberating effect on their scholarship.

The liberation early American scholars have sought is from that patriotic narrative that insistently accorded the United States an exceptional destiny even when, as with the Progressives, that destiny was used as a standard for calibrating shortcomings. With roots reaching deep into ancient Greece and medieval England, American institutions stood forth, in this account, as both climax and new beginning. As the organic

This chapter first appeared as "A Different Kind of Independence: The Postwar Restructuring of the Historical Study of Early America," *William and Mary Quarterly* 50, 3d ser. (April 1993): 245–67, and is reprinted with permission.

metaphor suggests, seeds once planted—be they town meetings or the practice of religious toleration—require only a favorable setting to come to fruition. And for many years historical scholarship on early America drew on this image of potent plantings in a uniquely favored environment to explain how a great nation emerged from a cluster of British colonies growing on the Atlantic shelf of North America. Trapped in this narrative structure, historians bestowed the lion's share of their attention on origins—origins of democratic practices, of religious liberty, of free enterprise, of the distinctive traits of American character.

Whether filiopietistic like most nineteenth-century studies or combative as in the Progressives' work, early American history remained fixed to the larger story of American nationhood. The generations of colonial life merged into a preparatory stage for the sequence of national events that began with the Revolution. And since the Revolution itself was treated as a precedent-shattering moment in world history, interest was always skewed toward the exceptional. Colonial heroes celebrated in schoolbooks were dissenters—men and some women out of step with their age because they were marching proleptically with the enlightened age that would give birth to the United States. Similarly, the charter colonists—always referred to as settlers rather than immigrants (one suspects a desire to differentiate them from the strange immigrants filling American cities)—were honored for their exceptional intrepidity. When Puritan magistrate William Stoughton announced that "God sifted a whole Nation that he might send choice Grain over into this wilderness," he provided a major leitmotif of Americans' self-understanding.[1]

After World War II, new scholarship undermined the Progressive interpretation of colonial society without displacing the central question of American historiography: how well were Americans keeping faith with their democratic promise? Spearheaded by Robert Brown's startling discovery that most adult white male colonists in Massachusetts could vote, scholarship supporting Brown's work directly challenged the facts on which the Progressives' view of a class-divided society had rested.[2] Brown's research led others—most notably Forrest McDonald and Daniel Boorstin—to complicate the category of interest groups and contest the predominating influence of economic factors.[3] In 1948, Carl Bridenbaugh bemoaned the "neglected first half of American History": a decade later, a freshet of new questions about colonial America had been released by Brown's provocative findings.[4] Freed from the Progressives' preoccupation with conflict, early American historians searched for the roots of American difference—but with a difference. Instead of focusing on an exceptional dispensation or divinely inspired destiny, they probed for the footings of social stability in general and asked how American conditions had promoted cooperation, coherence, and consensus. The thrusting and parrying between consensus historians and a band of neo-Progressives led by Merrill Jensen turned scholarly attention to social structure itself, a field of study that neo-Progressive Jackson Turner Main showed to be far more fertile than analysis of economic interest groups.[5]

The pathbreaking work of anthropologist Franz Boas and his brilliant students Margaret Mead and Ruth Benedict gave American scholars a quiver full of new arrows for studying society. With the protean concept of culture, historians could investigate the exceptional without disengaging from general theories about society.[6] Swift to gain ascendancy in postwar America, the emerging consensus synthesis prevailed for a surprisingly brief period, in part because it was difficult to contain the genuine curiosity stirred up by the effort to locate the cultural and structural components of American distinctiveness. The Progressives' critics recovered the consensual basis of colonial institutions and returned the period to its traditional "seedbed of democracy" orientation, to the undoubted relief of patriots. However, within ten years of the consolidation of the consensus school's interpretation, potent scholarly inquiries, emanating from France and England, burst on the academic scene, bringing colonial American scholars deliverance from their historiographical captivity within the "rise of the American nation" construction.

European academic influences promoted a new kind of social history—fresh in scope, style, topics, methods, and questions. The nature of society—its integrative mechanisms, its systems for distributing power, authority, and respect, its ideational repertoire—furnished the compelling questions for a new generation of historians. In taking up these themes, social historians—perhaps inadvertently—detached themselves and their scholarship from the Whiggish story of American progress that had absorbed their predecessors. Nowhere are the consequences of this metamorphosis of colonial scholarship better registered than in the books published by the Institute of Early American History and Culture and its celebrated third series of the *William and Mary Quarterly*. Nor could there be a better way to honor the institute's fiftieth anniversary than to revisit some of the intellectual sites where early American history won its interpretive autonomy.

In 1956, Fernand Braudel became editor of *Annales: Économies, societés, civilisations*, the journal around which a new school of French social historians was rallying. At the same time, across the channel, Peter Laslett organized the Cambridge Group for the Study of Population and Social Structure. Starting from different theoretical premises, both movements rustled the dry leaves of conventional scholarship by unleashing ambitious programs to recover the historic details of everyday life. Not far away in Cambridge, another group of scholars, gathered around Quentin Skinner and J. G. A. Pocock, began to examine the language of politics as a communicative system. These well-orchestrated research initiatives reflected a turning away from the older preoccupation with grand events, exceptional men, and transcendent ideas. Structure—a concept at odds with the American stress on individualism—entered scholarly discourse and revolutionized thinking about society, human nature, and the realm of meaning and purpose that mediated between the two. Like Tennyson's "flower in the crannied wall," ordinary life held out the promise of capturing the whole—in this case the whole of social existence.

Meanwhile, back in the United States, historians began to listen to the social scientists, who had been talking about structures and systems for some time. In 1958, the sociologist Talcott Parsons brought out an American edition of his 1947 translation of *The Protestant Ethic and the Spirit of Capitalism* by the grand theorist of Wilhelmine Germany, Max Weber. Building on Weber's understanding of how values bind and direct societies, Parsons developed a complex theory explaining the interaction of society's functions and structures. Parsonian structural-functionalism provided historians with ways to link social structure and political theory in order to explain stability, a topic rarely explored when progress hogged the spotlight. Similarly responsive to Weber was Clifford Geertz, whose aphoristic insights about group behavior introduced many intellectuals and scholars to the school of cultural anthropology founded by Boas. At the same time, the young Karl Marx was discovered by those eager to revamp orthodox Marxism with subtler renderings of values, language, and class consciousness. At long last, social scientists and historians began to speak the same language or, more accurately, learned to speak each other's.

The *Annalistes* sought nothing less than to comprehend past society in its totality.[7] Using a conceptual grid joining three levels of analysis to three units of time, Braudel rather dismissively consigned political history to the evanescent time span of mere events while celebrating the more enduring—and presumably more influential—category of the *longue durée* shaped by the environment. In between lay the medium term or *conjuncture*, where economic and social structures interconnected to form the historical context for change. Sharing the French enthusiasm for detailing the basic components of society, the Cambridge Group set out to capture the population dynamics of early modern England by reconstituting the families in several hundred parishes, a project that soon encompassed wide-ranging comparisons within and without Europe. Simultaneously, economic historians began to examine closely the agricultural systems on which population growth relied, while historical geographers looked anew at spatial mobility.[8]

By no means aloof from grand themes, *Annalistes* and Cambridge scholars were making a fresh assault on that Mount Everest of history and theory: explaining how a traditional Europe of limited productive capacity and limiting social prescriptions transformed itself into an expansive, innovating society growing exponentially with each new technological breakthrough. Highly relevant to the Cold War divide between socialist and free market societies, this question, which soon revealed itself as a nexus of interrelated questions, took off from the theoretical assertion of Marxism and liberalism, the one positing a revolutionary lurch from feudalism to capitalism, the other an evolutionary procession through hunting-and-gathering, pastoral, agricultural, and commercial stages. With their own universe divided among first, second, and third worlds, each grappling with complex problems of adaptation and innovation, postwar scholars found that their investigations bore a fascinating resemblance to current concerns about fundamental social change.

For American historians, the important fact about the new research program was that the arrows of inquiry started pointing toward the seventeenth and eighteenth centuries. As one of a network of locales intimately involved in the Atlantic exchange of peoples and goods, the colonies could be reconfigured as part of Western Europe. However, before early American historians could attach their subject to a larger European transformation, they had to rethink the notion of American exceptionalism. In part this was encouraged because new research on early modern Europe revealed that certain features of colonial life, such as geographic mobility and changes in inheritance laws, were evident on both sides of the Atlantic. More important, reconstructing the culture and structures of the diverse colonial societies within the context of newly discovered patterns of the Western world, offered an opportunity to look at American differences on a continuum instead of on a scale measuring progress.

This changed perspective made it easy to abandon the idea that what was truly important about the colonies was their contribution to American nationhood. Far from being a sacrifice, this stunning reconceptualization brought immediate benefits. Accepting the invitation to study colonial communities as microcosms of the early modern macrocosm connected early Americanists with the most vital centers of historical research in the West. In addition to this much-needed intellectual stimulus came the dividend of demonstrating the provinciality of one's predecessors. Muting the theme of American exceptionalism, colonial scholars recovered the cosmopolitanism of some of their seventeenth-century subjects.

Where earlier the technological wonders of the Industrial Revolution had dazzled scholars, now traditional patterns of living and working aroused curiosity as industrialization came to be understood as part of a longer process of economic change in which the values shaping family formation were as important as the marvelous machines that revolutionized textile manufacture. The objects of study switched from inventors and industrialists to copy-holding husbandmen and improving landlords as the period under investigation moved back a century and more. The careful reconstruction of peasant communities provided a checklist of everything that had to give way before industrialization was even feasible. Distanced ideologically from the notion of progress, historians could also ask whether industrialization was desirable and, if so, to whom.

The change of timing posed an interesting challenge to the historical imagination, for adjustments in population dynamics and agricultural productivity touched the most intimate rhythms and personal relations of customary life. The magnifying glass put to this patch of the past turned up exactly the kind of puzzles that promote research. It also revealed that the broad-brush interpretations associated with Marxist and classical liberal theories did not yield precise enough explanations about changes in farming techniques, price levels, and family reproductive strategies to satisfy the new investigators. With curiosity trained on the rupturing of traditional mores, many scholars turned to Weber, who had originally insisted that it was the spirit of capitalism, not the mechanics of investment and invention, that historians must explain.[9]

Investing the typical conditions of everyday existence with an importance they had never known before, historians made society—its geographic setting, its enduring traditions, its productive and reproductive activities—the central focus of historical research. Rebaptized as early modern communities, the American colonies became testing grounds for a battery of intriguing hypotheses about social change. With these came new methodologies. Reconstructing the lives of ordinary people entailed the painstaking process of sifting through long record runs of births, marriages, deaths, wills, and land transfers—data sets, as we learned to call them. Two developments promoted these time-consuming studies: the expansion of higher education from the 1950s vastly increased the number of men and women looking for dissertation topics, and the introduction of the computer greatly facilitated the quantitative analysis of vital records. This omnibus of talents, techniques, and theses carried the colonial period into the academic fast lane by which it made good its escape from an earlier concentration on the foundations of American nationhood. Because the vast expansion of higher education brought women and minorities into the mainstream professions, social historians—often the first in their families to become academics—found a ready audience among their students for their writings on the character of ordinary life, the origins of slavery, the radical impulses in popular religion, and the structuring of power and status. The democratization of higher education, with poetic justice, delivered on the promise of democratic scholarship by producing an unparalleled richness of information about the past lives of ordinary men and women.

Primed to investigate agricultural practices, inheritance patterns, and the organization of local government, scholars first took advantage of the wealth of records in New England towns. The initial seeding of this fertile ground produced a bumper crop with the publication in 1970 of Philip Greven, *Four Generations*; Kenneth Lockridge, *A New England Town*; John Demos, *A Little Commonwealth*; and Michael Zuckerman, *Peaceable Kingdoms*.[10] As if to underscore the significance of this bonanza of community studies, major learned journals invited review essays of these books, thus enabling astute critics such as Rhys Isaac, James Henretta, John Murrin, Richard Dunn, and Jack Greene to take stock of the firstfruits of the cross-fertilization of demography and local history.[11] Where pioneering works from Sumner Chilton Powell, Darrett Rutman, and Richard Bushman had emphasized the contentions in early New England, the new studies drew a picture of the social dynamics of consensus.

The studies of New England towns documented as never before the efforts of settlers to knit themselves into tight little communitarian worlds. Braiding the complementary strands of English local government, Puritan worship, and household economies into a distinctive form of life, these colonists created inward-looking communities of remarkable internal cohesion and life-nurturing prosperity. What the careful reconstitution of births, marriages, and deaths revealed was the pivotal importance of the family, an institution that infused both meaning and motives into individual lives while creating a social base that was both material and moral. These studies proved fascinating to readers long sated by the celebratory descriptions of liberal dissenters and freethinking mavericks. They demonstrated as well the appeal of the colonial era in its own right, disconnected from the story of the American nation that was to come.

Among its many blessings, historical demography provided an analytical purchase for research on ordinary people. Ordinary people had been studied before but without social scientific models that linked their lives to the emergence of capitalism and the transformation of society. Social history had been peripheral to the dominant narrative of progressive political development. Nowhere was this new accession of centrality more apparent than in the treatment of women, whose reproductive records figured prominently in family reconstitution. Teased from the parish records was information about childbearing, dower rights, and prenuptial arrangements that gave precision to the family strategies of early modern couples. Again the hypotheses generated by social science models offered a way to move beyond anecdote to the structural features of society. With sustained research on the distaff side of colonial life, talk of intergeneric intervals and age at menarche found its way into conference papers and monographs, thus giving women a vivid physical presence that cried out for social elaboration. Two works in 1980, Mary Beth Norton's *Liberty's Daughters* and Linda Kerber's *Women of the Republic*, pioneered in linking microscopic data to macroscopic events—in both cases the American Revolution.[12]

Developing simultaneously with an intensely passionate reassessment of women's place in present-day society, this scholarship flourished under the guidance of feminist theory that pushed questions about male power and social control to the fore. Having said good-bye to the archetypal American—the mobile and intrepid individual seeking religious freedom and economic advancement in the New World—historians had to make the acquaintance of the devout and confident community-oriented patriarch. Similarly, colonial women had to be viewed against the foreground figure of this new mate, and while the lineaments of the colonial householder and his sons became sharper, those of his spouse and his daughters were draped in controversy. The colonial era had once been considered their golden age when shortages of women promoted better marriages and more favorable standing before the law. Training a research magnifying glass on the details of ordinary life provided a wealth of new information along with contradictory evaluations of it. Legal historians traced the confinements of common-law coverture and followed angry women as plaintiffs and defendants.[13] Historians of religion tracked their conversions, church attendance, and apostasies.[14] The prominence of women in Salem's witchcraft trials provoked a succession of interpretations, none more electrifying in its connections of status, deviance, and power than Carol Karlsen's *The Devil in the Shape of a Woman*.[15] Exploiting women's journals and diaries, Richard and Joy Buel, Nancy Cott, and Laurel Thatcher Ulrich recovered the qualitative richness of women's lives that eludes quantitative studies.[16]

The concept of culture has helped scholars destabilize or problematize the concreteness of sexual differences. Women's historians have drawn on current theoretical work to subvert our sense of the givenness of the subordination of women by detailing the specific arrangements affecting women's lives. In this they were helped by feminist use of the word "gender," shed of its exclusively grammatical reference, to denote the social construction of female attributes. The idea of *histoire totale* carried with it the assumption of a structural integrity in society that women's history has repeatedly confirmed. Every new finding about one sex has generated knowledge about the other and about the gender roles that mediate their interaction. Nowhere is this better demonstrated than in Ruth Bloch's and Jan Lewis's explorations of the fascinating ways in which the vocabulary and theatrics of gender impinged on the political language of republicanism.[17]

In his review of the 1970 crop of New England town studies, Jack Greene commented that seventeenth- and eighteenth-century Anglo-Americans would have been surprised by the amount of attention bestowed on New England in contrast to the Caribbean sugar and Chesapeake tobacco colonies. Moreover, he argued, the behavioral revolution that eventually turned the obedient members of corporate communities into the self-assertive, property-oriented individuals we know as Americans could better be traced beyond the reach of Puritanism.[18] The settlements of Virginia and Maryland, after all, had been attuned from the outset to the imperatives of that Atlantic trade world that was slowly transforming the low-yield, demographically precarious agrarian order of Europe. Far from the metropolitan center, what Eric McKitrick and Stanley Elkins called the "dynamics of unopposed capitalism" were shaping a dramatically different society on the periphery.[19]

Since town records had kept the engine of social history going for New England, it is not surprising that the pioneering archival work of Lois Green Carr at the St. Mary's City Commission led to a burgeoning of research on the Chesapeake. Starting like the New England scholars with historical demography, Carr, Lorena Walsh, Russell Menard, Anita and Darrett Rutman, Gloria Main, Michael Harris, Edward Papenfuse, Gregory Stiverson, Allan Kulikoff, Paul Clemens, and others exploited the riches of probate inventories, orphan's courts, and land titles to portray a vastly different colonial society in which sickness predominated over health and dispersion made the county rather than the community the focal point of colonists' communal lives.[20] Working with settlers less articulate in their social purposes than the Puritans, historians of the Chesapeake showed how thoroughly their sophisticated statistical analyses of local records could extract information. From this work came the stark demonstration of the differences in the life chances of those English and African men and women whose New World was an encounter with diseases, foods, and people utterly foreign to them. Similarly, the fine sieve of statistical analysis made possible highly refined interpretations of social stratification as well as of responses to market cues, especially the farmers' switch from tobacco to wheat. The historical demography that uncovered the unprecedented longevity of New England patriarchs uncovered just as effectively the population catastrophes that marked the early Chesapeake.

Slavery above all distinguished the culture of the Chesapeake from that of New England, and the research that clarified the genesis of American slavery developed along a different route from that of community studies. Like other topics forced into prominence by World War II, race prejudice became too salient a feature of social life to be ignored by historians. In 1950, in a justly famous article, Oscar and Mary Handlin presented findings about early Virginia that suggested that slavery generated race prejudice instead of the reverse.[21] It is difficult today to recapture the cognitive dissonance such a proposition created, so accustomed were Americans to relying on innate prejudice to explain the ugliness of their race relations. In the fruitful exchange that followed, two arguments were advanced—the one emphasizing how English reactions to African Americans promoted slavery, the other historicizing the origins of the colonists' peculiar institution. Relying on a small group of documents that pointed to the indeterminacy of the status of the first Africans in Virginia, the Handlins, Carl Degler, and Winthrop Jordan explored how social attitudes and contingent opportunities played on the decisions that fixed or unfixed the labor systems of the southern colonies.[22] As in the best scholarly debates, the research of such historians as Menard, Kulikoff, Philip Morgan, Timothy Breen, Stephen Innes, and Edmund Morgan forced a broadening of the argument.[23]

By the time Morgan wrote *American Slavery, American Freedom*, the fruits of twenty-five years of searching analysis had become evident. Discussions of the origins of slavery could no longer pivot on race prejudice and an ill-defined need for labor. Historians knew too much about the impact of mortality rates, information flows, price levels, immigration trends, international rivalries, local politics, and the character of Virginia's charter planters. The *Annalistes'* summons to study the totality of past societies had called forth a nearly inexhaustible inquisitiveness in researchers who learned to squeeze information from previously inert sources. Imaginatively using the tools of anthropology, Peter Wood, John Blassingame, Isaac, Mechal Sobel, and others invested the social historians' quantitative analyses with the "thick description" of people's lives.[24] The benefits of this new work were as much moral as intellectual, for it is one thing to know that there is an institution called slavery but quite another to identify with the slaves' experience by learning the dimensions of their living space, the traditions they brought from diverse parts of Africa, and the patterns of work and respite that defined the terms of survival in the cruelest of labor systems.

There was an essential conservatism to research that focused on family reconstitutions and agricultural practices. Both projects located people in venerable systems of production and reproduction. At the same time, the cutting edge of American social history was being sharpened on the left. Ordinary people had been objects of inquiry for radical scholars since the Progressives introduced embattled farmers, debtors, workers, and westerners into the historical consciousness of the nation. Ordinary people locked in combat with their social superiors, whether aristocratic planters or oligarchic mill owners, personified American democracy perennially put at risk by economic trends promoting inequality. If demographic studies outside the South were more likely to capture continuity and stability, colonial cities, with their conspicuous differentiation of rank and hotly contested elections, offered a better locale for studying political conflict in early America, as the work of such historians as Jesse Lemisch, Gary Nash, Eric Foner, and Alfred Young demonstrated.[25]

Driven by a passion to give voice to the inarticulate, a cohort of social historians developed a rationale and an agenda for writing history from the bottom up. Exploiting records detailing the life patterns of artisans, occasional laborers, sailors, and the recipients of charity, the resulting scholarship provided the empirical basis for assessing trends in mobility, standards of living, employment, and wealth distribution while at the same time introducing Jack Tars, leather aprons, and White Oaks into their narratives. Moving far beyond the Progressives' concern with class-based politics, social historians attended to the ways in which ethnicity, evangelicalism, and artisanal culture gave meaning to working-class lives while promoting group action.[26] In a resurgence of Marxist scholarship,

British historians E. P. Thompson, George Rudé, Eric Hobsbawm, and Christopher Hill moved beyond meaning to means of expression and provided Americans with potent models for bringing to light how lower-class men and women actively pursued their goals. The popular presence in the American Revolution that Progressives tended to ascribe to upper-class propaganda became for neo-Progressives such as Edward Countryman, Dirk Hoerder, Joseph Ernst, Ronald Hoffman, Ira Berlin, and Nash evidence of the Revolution's genuinely radical potential.[27]

The most significant casualty of the New Social History has been the idea that America was born free, rich, and modern. Instead of traveling light to the New World, the original settlers brought a full complement of cultural baggage and succeeded against odds—at least in New England—in reconstituting the familiar patterns of their homeland. Indeed, new scholarship has nearly reversed the conventional contrast between old regime Europe moving away from customary ways at glacial speed and newly minted America giving currency to every passing innovation. Extended life spans enabled New England patriarchs to preside longer over the lives of their adult children than in Europe, and members of the colonial elite everywhere strove to imitate English forms and fashions with the mimetic urgency of true provincials. As Murrin has indicated, enhanced prosperity in the eighteenth century inspired Anglicization—the process through which the colonists consciously patterned their clothes, their manners, and their homes after those of the mother country.[28] Yet if America was not born liberal, it certainly became so, and discovering when and how remains crucial to the historiography of American democracy and its economic relative, capitalism.

In something of a scholar's conundrum, the discrediting of the concept of progress actually intensified an interest in change. Only the terms of change vastly changed, pushing scholars to ask how members of a traditional society had ever acquired the social attributes of modernity. The sustained rupture of customary ways that produced modern society took place in the seventeenth and eighteenth centuries, yet our understanding of the modern transformation lags behind the accretion of information. Price levels and wealth distribution can be patiently teased from longitudinal data sets; how people choose to respond to new situations is less easily reconstructed from the records. The success of the first made more urgent study of the second, for the accumulation of research increasingly points to the fact that behind the articulation of market networks lay market planning and behind that cognitive terra incognita operated the invisible influences of social values and personal character. Comparison among towns and regions similarly reveals the unreliability of mechanical explanations of social change because of the varied responses to population growth and commercial novelties. Only an interrogation about values and attitudes, stripped of anticipations of the future, can make salient the cultural meaning participants found in economic innovations.

In the opening shot of what proved to be a lively battle about the origins of American capitalism, Henretta argued that northern farmers were oriented toward the preservation of their lineal family and not to the opportunities for economic advance held out by enlarging trade.[29] Drawing on the growing body of community studies, Henretta described a web of social relationships spun among farm families that inhibited the play of market forces, which, he further maintained, only penetrated rural communities late in the eighteenth century. His either-or framing of the question invigorated both critics and sympathizers. The historical geographer James Lemon, whose work on colonial Pennsylvania had prompted Henretta's article in the first place, took issue by insisting that the English settlers had brought to America the acquisitive attitudes of the economically advanced mother country.[30] Colonial leaders, Lemon wrote, were active agents of change whose entrepreneurial ethos flourished in the more permissive environment of the New World. They were animated by the desire to accumulate property for profit, prestige, and power, according to Lemon, and became the objects of emulation among ordinary colonists.

The research that both scholars were interpreting had shown that, despite the power of the community, relentless forces of change kept beating against the institutions that sheltered northern farm families. The decline of mortality led to overpopulation, which in turn translated into the outmigration of sons and daughters; religious wrangling fragmented congregations; and the impersonal force of the market and the personal authority of a distant monarch had intruded on New England's "peaceable kingdoms." To understand the commodification of land, labor, and savings that exemplified capitalism, historians had to join the close examination of prices, wages, and interest rates with longitudinal community studies. Following the American economy well into the nineteenth century offered the best prospect for getting behind market changes to the behavior that prompted them.

Spurred by the enlarging database for early American farms and the increasing sophistication of statistical analysis, historians began to examine the northern rural economy in light of the Henretta–Lemon debate. Inferring social responses from the changing costs of labor, goods, and loans, as well as the household strategies revealed in wills and account books, Christopher Clark, John Brooke, Bettye Hobbs Pruitt, Winifred Rothenberg, Stephen Innes, Mary Schweitzer, and others demonstrated the power of microscopic studies to refine and redirect broad interpretive questions.[31] Much of the intentionality previously imputed to innovating entrepreneurs or tradition-affirming conservatives was replaced by an appreciation of the middle ground where men and women pursued goals through a succession of short-range decisions, many of which entailed unintended long-range consequences. Because of the durability of structures, a number of historians have carried their research across the line dividing colonial and early national history, revealing at the same time a different set of connections between the colonies and the nation to be. In an important article, "Competency and Competition: Economic Culture in Early America," Daniel Vickers explored a central irony of life—people always move into an unknown future with values deeply rooted in the past—and clarified how conservative values could themselves facilitate radical change.[32]

Simultaneously during the 1960s and 1970s, historians began to examine the social forms of African and Amerindian peoples whose existence had been cast into the shadows by the searchlight trained on the carriers of Western advance. Inspired by the anthropological studies of Boas and Clyde Kluckhohn, they profited from the quickening of interest in non-Western cultures that came with the diminished credibility of the West's claims to be directing the path of human destiny. Without the teleology of progress, social scientists stopped ranking societies according to their approximation to modern Western norms, a practice that became more a curiosity of nineteenth-century Western hubris than a useful organizing tool. As Jacques Derrida shrewdly observed, ethnology could only have been born as a science after the "de-centering" of European culture itself.[33] Derrida's remark underscores the connection between the broad-based philosophical attack on Western philosophy and the stirring of historical sympathies for the groups that were outside the charmed circle of democratic progress.

Quick to appreciate the pedagogical opening of this de-centering, Nash in *Red, White, and Black: The Peoples of Early America* reoriented college students to colonial history by beginning with the three racial groups contending for space, resources, recognition, and power on the North American continent.[34] More provocatively, Francis Jennings, in *The Invasion of America*, excoriated what he called the "cant of conquest" by analyzing the linguistic devices through which English settlers had obscured their initial dependence on Amerindian accomplishments.[35] These deconstructions of the West's ideological pretensions invited historians to study Native Americans with the sympathetic curiosity formerly reserved for the colonists, a move made more easily because the colonial period was attracting historical curiosity independent of interest in American nationhood.

Ethnology, with its attentiveness to the coherence and meaning permeating each group's practical and symbolic enactments, gave historians a powerful methodology for studying the tribal societies of North America as well as the African traditions transplanted in the New World.[36] Not allowing the knowledge of eventual Indian removal to cloud their perception of the original encounters, such historians as James Axtell, James Merrell, James Ronda, Neal Salisbury, and Daniel Richter have added experiential depth to the meaning of contact between the Europeans and the Eastern tribes of native Americans.[37] In seeking to articulate the reasoning and purposes underpinning the Indians' work, worship, and understanding of the human condition, these scholars recreated the most fascinating of all frontiers, the ones where men and women confront the fact of otherness. By analyzing the interracial encounters at the Atlantic beachheads of European expansion, they have not only restored the Indian presence but have also developed another angle of vision on the history of American race relations.

Deprived of a belief in progress, historians could entertain the idea that men and women in the seventeenth and eighteenth centuries might actually have been indifferent or even hostile to the novelties that were incessantly reconfiguring the world they inherited. Perhaps the creative destruction that economist Joseph Schumpeter called the hallmark of capitalism produced more anxiety about its destructiveness than admiration for its creativity. With an élan that intellectual historians rarely display, Pocock pursued these speculations. Inspiring the most thorough revision in early American studies of the past quarter century, that of the republican synthesis, he propelled the study of past thought toward the same conceptual vortex that was simultaneously acting on social history—the discovery of structure.[38] Concentrating initially on political language as a system that distributes significance and power, Pocock pioneered a strategy for scholars that avoided both the self-congratulatory sentimentalism of great ideas and the mindless unmasking of economic determinism.[39] Whereas Marxists had rooted political thought in the tactical imperatives of upper-class social control and humanists had connected it with the universal search for truth under the guidance of reason, Pocock historicized it. He began with the proposition that languages become codes as people acquire and refine a collective understanding of reality. Hence historians, as decoders, must be deeply familiar with the highly particular meanings of the references and metaphors in a given community of speakers.

In providing a vehicle for cultural meaning, language, Pocock argued, both directs and inhibits individual actions and hence becomes an important component in the exercise of political authority. Instead of studying individuals and the ideas they articulated, the new ideological historians highlighted the ways that societies construct "reality" through shared discourses. Where Whig history had assumed that human nature endowed men with an independent capacity to size up reality, ideology— a concept that refers to the structuring of thinking—encloses human consciousness within a social skein of organized reasoning.

The particular structured reality that Pocock and others discovered in the eighteenth-century Anglo-American world was informed by classical republican ideas gleaned from ancient texts as they passed through Renaissance hands. Bernard Bailyn, working with much the same sociological theory in his analysis of pamphlets of the American Revolution, elevated ideology to causal preeminence. The ideology he found animating American pamphlets was that of the English opposition that had popularized classical republicanism in its public indictment of the abuse of power by Britain's Whig magnates.[40] The republican synthesis carried the transformation of early American historiography well beyond the colonial period, for it advanced an interpretation of the colonists' beliefs and hence of their reality that transformed scholarly understanding of the Revolution, the Constitution, and the formation of political parties in the 1790s.[41] These nation-building acts were no longer the work of radicals, but, as Gordon Wood powerfully demonstrated, of conservative men embedded in the interlocking structures of ideas and institutions that their colonial predecessors had successfully transplanted.[42] Reborn as classical republicans—nervous about what was coming and nostalgic about the civilized order in retreat—eighteenth-century Americans at last became strangers to twentieth-century readers long used to being on familiar terms with their forebears.

The republican revision had grown out of the aggressive testing of Brown's assertion that early America was a middle-class democracy. Studying colonial political writings, Caroline Robbins, Edmund and Helen Morgan, Cecelia Kenyon, Roy Lokken, J. R. Pole, and others discovered an intellectual world that bore little resemblance to the modern middle-class ethos described by consensus historians.[43] A fruitful puzzle emerged: why did ordinary men who possessed the vote help maintain a hierarchical order that stressed the critical political distinction between the few and the many? Under the pressure of this conundrum, assumptions about a universal craving for freedom and equality collapsed and the concept of culture—particularly the idea of deference—was brought in to explain why the colonists were not agents of progress, prescient modernists, or purposeful founders of the United States. For Pocock, Bailyn, and Wood, the colonists reasoned within a classical republican logic that linked the British imperial reforms of the 1760s and 1770s to Renaissance teachings about the state. Precipitated into independence, the revolutionary elite adapted civic humanist values to the exigencies of a social situation that they were just discovering to be utterly different from that of England.

This ideological interpretation of the Revolution involved both a theory about how ideas enter into history and empirical findings about which ideas American leaders espoused. By stressing that all thinking is mediated through socially articulated understandings of reality, the republican synthesis gave causal force to an ornate classical ideal about the constitutional balance between the few and the many. It was not just that American spokesmen took their political bearings from a civic humanist understanding of state and society but that, having constructed their reality, these ideas remained to influence political choices for the next thirty years. What gave structure such salience in this explanation was the psychological assertion that the articulate mind of the colonists had been wired so that certain signals—in this case, the succession of imperial tax and reform measures—produced particular behavioral reactions, that is, looked like assaults on colonial liberties and hence provoked resistance.[44] The explanatory power of the republican revision depended on the concept of structure: ideas enter history not as separate thoughts to be weighed by autonomous thinkers but as constituent elements in a social construction of reality that determines how men and women interpret events, assign value, and decide to act.

Republicanism became the most important organizing idea for the history of the early national period because it shed light on the conflicts between supporters and opponents of the Constitution, Jeffersonians and Federalists, and, more generally, the entrepreneurs, artisans, and farmers of the early republic.[45] True to the Braudelian sense of structure, the colonial past was seen as casting a long shadow over the *histoire événementielle* of the new nation. The plausibility of this strong revision of the standing wisdom about the Founding Fathers owed much to the social historians' recovery of the traditionalism lodged in the colonists' familial and community life. At the same time, other intellectual historians began to doubt the paradigmatic force of Renaissance civic humanism, and their skepticism precipitated a protracted debate about the conceptual languages available to America's revolutionary leaders.[46] Dissenting scholars pointed out that despite efforts to replicate the social forms of the Old World in the New, the British American colonies were outposts of an ambitious and innovative European power more interested in cultivating enterprise than piety. Radical notions about the state had been a marked feature of England's century of revolution, some scholars noted, and many of these notions had taken root in the colonies along with classical republicanism and variants of Christian millennialism. Such findings undermined much of the force of the republican synthesis because it had relied on a single dominant intellectual paradigm to explain why colonial leaders interpreted parliamentary taxation in a particular way. With critics detailing the multitude of political languages available to the colonists, the issue of choice pressed to the fore. Open once more was the old question of what social factors disposed men and women to think in which ways. Like so many earlier organizing themes in American historiography, the wildfire success of republicanism began to illuminate contemporary concerns of historians more than the past, demonstrating anew the special tensions present when writing the history of one's own country.

Few intellectual endeavors thrive in a straitjacket, and the study of early America was no exception. It could produce institutional histories of meticulous detail like those of Herbert Baxter Adams's students. It could follow, Hegel-like, the germ of an idea as it bore fruit in mature intellectual traditions like the constitutional studies of Charles McIlwain. It could critique the inflated claims of its own historiographical tradition as in Wesley Frank Craven's writings on the Virginia Company. What it could not do before the 1960s was stop playing pedestal to the Revolution's statue. Two major exceptions to this generalization are Charles McLean Andrews and Perry Miller, both deeply immersed in the larger European context in which the colonists worked and thought.[47] While Andrews's interest in local institutions and imperial administration did not resonate with the next generation of scholars, Miller's study of Puritanism spoke directly to the postwar fascination with structure, in this case the mirroring structures of a highly sophisticated theology and the civil and religious institutions it informed. Defining himself in opposition to the prevailing historiography of the 1930s and 1940s, Miller extolled the power of mind over matter as he demonstrated how the Puritans imposed intentions on the material circumstances of their new home. More impressed with the trickle down of powerful ideas expounded by forceful leaders than by the bubble up of popular enthusiasms, Miller nonetheless influenced the generation of social historians who painstakingly reconstructed the family strategies, cropping techniques, and inheritance patterns of Puritan families by providing a world of meaning for their subjects.

The attention given to what the sociologists Peter Berger and Thomas Luckmann call the craving for meaning inevitably led colonial historians to a reevaluation of religion.[48] Miller's work was a beacon, and cultural anthropology a map, for the integration of religious history into the mainstream scholarly categories of political, economic, and social developments. The recovery of the language of religion meant the acquisition of the words and concepts that the colonists themselves used to make sense of their lives. The abandonment of the interpretive framework of progress also meant that secularization could be dropped as a kind of terminus toward which early American societies were moving. Miller's Puritanism offered a paradigm for New England studies that, in the sense in which Thomas Kuhn had described the function of paradigms, prescribed the broad areas of "normal science" for the field.[49] The lexicon that Miller appropriated from his subject—declension, jeremiad, errand, covenant, piety, typology—furnished the terms with which later scholars discussed the corporate identity that Puritans forged around the narrative of an errand into the wilderness to build a city on a hill. Miller's work became the departure point for thinking about colonial religion, although it was by no means accepted unquestioningly by Puritan scholars like David Hall, Stephen Foster, Robert Middlekauff, Michael McGiffert, Charles Hambrick-Stowe, Norman Fiering, Norman Pettit, Harry Stout, E. Brooks Holifield, and Charles Cohen.[50] In following the lead of Hall, Jon Butler, and Patricia Bonomi toward the study of popular religion, recent work had forged new linkages between social structure and cultural meaning and has drawn scholars into further fruitful exchanges with European students of religion.[51]

Scholars beginning their careers in the 1950s did so against the background of a devastating world war preceded by the ravages of world depression. The hatreds unleashed by fascism cruelly mocked Western assumptions about the unfolding of political and economic advance. Not even scientific truth emerged from the war unscathed, for the ever-ascending achievements of physics unexpectedly culminated in the threat of global destruction. An abrupt closure interrupted the seamless story of progress. The modern era had acquired an end point; in the wings was the nomenclature of "post"—postindustrial, postmodern, postempirical, poststructural. Expectations of economic development and social progress, for which modernization theory briefly offered an explanation, were repeatedly dashed by failed "takeoffs" and renewed expressions of ethnic particularities and religious fundamentalism. No sooner had social theory accommodated the permanence of "underdevelopment" with a new theory about the structured dominance of core over periphery than countries in the denominated periphery unexpectedly began to industrialize. The center was not holding nor was the center's intellectual apparatus.[52]

Under this battering from events, assumptions about the West's mastery of social process could no longer avoid examination. Exposed too was the way that the teleology of progress had influenced historical scholarship. A host of provocative questions assailed the cohort of scholars who tried to make sense of the past in the light of the vast accretion of social information garnered in the second half of the twentieth century. It became apparent that the grand theses of the nineteenth century—those brilliant extrapolations from Adam Smith, Karl Marx, and Charles Darwin—provided theoretical answers that no longer satisfied curiosities fed by an additional century of human experience. More specifically, by portraying human history as interlocking processes guided by unvarying mechanisms—division of labor, class conflict, survival of the fittest—these theses were tied to a paradigm that was unraveling. New what-ifs could be imagined. If the hegemony of the West is not written into the script of world history, how can one account for the undoubted modernity of Western Europe and the United States? The dawning awareness of the failure of metahistory produced an urgent, even excited cognizance of all the questions that had not been posed about the transition from a world of small, custom-bound, materially restricted localities to one of rich and powerful nations with complex, differentiated institutions reaching toward new global integration.

Historians thrive on such speculation. Always in the center of the nation's intellectual life, they do not stand outside, studying the past from some disinterested vantage point. The passionate engagements of the day are theirs; the arresting contemporary questions are the ones they use to interrogate the records. In the past half century, history has been particularly pertinent to major inquiries as our certainty about grand theories diminishes, leaving us to replot the trajectory of human aspiration independent of inexorable trends. National identity is also implicated in historical scholarship, for what we think we are as a nation is intimately linked with how we understand what we have done and believed as a people. Collective memory and reconstructed memory fuse in the popular imagination, leaving historians to redraw the boundaries among myth, fantasy, factual record, and grand interpretation. The past fifty years have tightened the bond between history and contemporary issues because, since World War II ended, the compelling questions—those posed about technological change, cultural meaning, racial attitudes, multicultural identities, nationalism, and the ends of social existence—have led ineluctably back to the past.

No longer the custodians of colonial origins and liberal heroes, historians of early America have reconstructed ways of living and thinking quite different from those that triumphed after the Revolution. Roads not taken, acorns that did not produce oaks, are now in view. Possibilities abound. If the historical intellect cannot accurately predict where we are going, it can at least bring imagination and commitment to the exploration of where we have been. In the case of early American history, there is a principal irony in the field's seeking conceptual autonomy in the embrace of the social sciences. The models of structure that help organize quantitative research provided hypotheses that, once tested, revealed the need to know more about human agency. Meaning, interpretation, discourse, intentionality—the full repertoire of ascendently human achievements—represent the obscured reality that historians want to grasp. Ordinary lives, far from revealing ordinary endeavors, have become the focal points for fascinating investigations of how human beings construct identity, transcend suffering, and create existential narratives. For the future, early American historians have a full agenda, continuing the assault on that Mount Everest of social change while enlarging the sympathies of their contemporaries with the stories of neglected participants. Their liberation from a patriotically inspired parochialism has gained for them and their readers a new world of experience.

NOTES

1. Quoted in Perry Miller, *The New England Mind: From Colony to Province* (Cambridge, Mass., 1953), 135.

2. Brown, *Middle-Class Democracy and the Revolution in Massachusetts, 1691–1780* (Ithaca, N.Y., 1955); and Brown and B. Katherine Brown, *Virginia, 1705–1786: Democracy or Aristocracy?* (East Lansing, Mich., 1964).

3. McDonald, *We the People: The Economic Origins of the Constitution* (Chicago, 1958); Daniel Boorstin, *The Americans: The Colonial Experience* (New York, 1958); Louis Hartz, *The Liberal Tradition in America: An Interpretation of American Political Thought since the Revolution* (New York, 1955).

4. Bridenbaugh, "The Neglected First Half of American History," *American Historical Review* 53 (1947–1948): 506–17.

5. Jensen, *The New Nation* (New York, 1950); Main, *The Social Structure of Revolutionary America* (Princeton, 1965); and Main, *Political Parties before the Constitution* (Chapel Hill, N.C., 1973).

6. A fine overview of this development is given in Robert F. Berkhofer Jr., "Clio and the Culture Concept: Some Impressions of a Changing Relationship in American Historiography," in Louis Schneider and Charles M. Bonjean, eds., *The Idea of Culture in the Social Sciences* (Cambridge, Mass., 1973), 77–100.

7. Marc Bloch and Lucien Febvre founded *Annales d'histoire économique et sociale* in 1929. Renamed *Annales: Économique, sociétés, civilisations*, the journal was moved to Paris after the war, with Braudel as its editor. For a history of the *Annales* school, see Traian Stoianovich, *French Historical Method: The Annales Paradigm* (Ithaca, N.Y., 1976).

8. R. M. Hartwell, "Economic Growth in England before the Industrial Revolution: Some Methodological Issues," *Journal of Economic History* 29 (1969): 13–31; J. D. Gould, *Economic Growth in History* (London, 1972); E. A. Wrigley, "A Simple Model of London's Importance in Changing English Society and Economy, 1650–1750," *Past and Present* 37 (1967): 44–70.

9. Weber, *The Protestant Ethic and the Spirit of Capitalism*, trans. Talcott Parsons (1947; New York, 1958).

10. Greven, *Four Generations: Population, Land, and Family in Colonial Andover, Massachusetts* (Ithaca, N.Y., 1970); Lockridge, *A New England Town, the First Hundred Years: Dedham, Massachusetts, 1636–1736* (New York, 1970); Demos, *A Little Commonwealth: Family Life in Plymouth Colony* (New York, 1970); Zuckerman, *Peaceable Kingdoms: New England Towns in the Eighteenth Century* (New York, 1970). Less focused on demography but exploring the social history of particular locales were Sumner Chilton Powell, *Puritan Village: The Formation of a New England Town* (Middletown, Conn., 1963); Darrett B. Rutman, *Winthrop's Boston: Portrait of a Puritan Town, 1630–1649* (Chapel Hill, N.C., 1965); and Richard L. Bushman, *From Puritan to Yankee: Character and the Social Order in Connecticut, 1690–1765* (Cambridge, Mass., 1967).

11. Isaac, "Order and Growth, Authority and Meaning in Colonial New England," *American Historical Review* 76 (1971): 728–37; Henretta, "The Morphology of New England Society in the Colonial Period," *Journal of Interdisciplinary History* 2 (1971–1972): 379–98; Murrin, "Review Essay," *History and Theory* 11 (1972): 226–75; Dunn, "The Social History of Early New England," *American Quarterly* 24 (1972): 661–79; Greene, "Autonomy and Stability: New England and the British Colonial Experience in Early Modern America," *Journal of Social History* 7 (1973–1974): 171–94.

12. Kerber, *Women of the Republic: Intellect and Ideology in Revolutionary America* (Chapel Hill, N.C., 1980); Norton, *Liberty's Daughters: The Revolutionary Experience of American Women, 1750–1800* (Boston, 1980).

13. Marylynn Salmon, *Women and the Law of Property in Early America* (Chapel Hill, N.C., 1986); and Lyle Koehler, *A Search for Power: The "Weaker Sex" in Seventeenth-Century New England* (Urbana, Ill., 1980).

14. Christine Leigh Heyrman, *Commerce and Culture: The Maritime Communities of Colonial Massachusetts, 1690–1750* (New York, 1984); Carla Gardina Pestana, *Quakers and Baptists in Colonial Massachusetts* (New York, 1991); Koehler, *A Search for Power;* Patricia U. Bonomi, *Under the Cope of Heaven: Religion, Society, and Politics in Colonial America* (Oxford, 1986).

15. Karlsen, *The Devil in the Shape of a Woman: Witchcraft in Colonial New England* (New York, 1987).

16. Buel and Buel, *The Way of Duty: A Woman and Her Family in Revolutionary America* (New York, 1984); Cott, *The Bonds of Womanhood: "Woman's Sphere" in New England, 1780–1835* (New Haven, Conn., 1977); Laurel Thatcher Ulrich, *A Midwife's Tale: The Life of Martha Ballard, Based on Her Diary, 1785–1812* (New York, 1991).

17. Bloch, "The Gendered Meanings of Virtue in Revolutionary America," *Signs: Journal of Women in Culture and Society* 13 (1987–1988); and Lewis, "The Republican Wife: Virtue and Seduction in the Early Republic," *William and Mary Quarterly,* 3d ser., 46 (1987): 689–721.

18. Greene, "Autonomy and Stability," 172–73. Greene fully developed these ideas in *Pursuits of Happiness: The Social Development of Early Modern British Colonies and the Formation of American Culture* (Chapel Hill, N.C., 1988).

19. Elkins and McKitrick, "Institutions and the Law of Slavery: The Dynamics of Unopposed Capitalism," *American Quarterly* 9 (1957): 3–21.

20. Carr, Philip D. Morgan, and Jean B. Russo, eds., *Colonial Chesapeake Society* (Chapel Hill, N.C., 1988); Aubrey C. Land, Carr, and Papenfuse, eds., *Land, Society, and Politics in Early Maryland* (Baltimore, 1977); Gloria Main, *Tobacco Colony: Life in Early Maryland, 1650–1720* (Princeton, 1982); Stiverson, *Poverty in a Land of Plenty: Tenancy in Eighteenth-Century Maryland* (Baltimore, 1977); Kulikoff, *Tobacco and Slaves: The Development of Southern Cultures in the Chesapeake, 1680–1800* (Chapel Hill, N.C., 1986); Clemens, *The Atlantic Economy and Colonial Maryland's Eastern Shore: From Tobacco to Grain* (Ithaca, N.Y., 1980). See also Anita Rutman, "Still Planting the Seeds of Hope: The Recent Literature of the Early Chesapeake Region," *Virginia Magazine of History and Biography* 95 (1987): 3–24.

21. Handlin and Handlin, "Origins of the Southern Labor System," *William and Mary Quarterly,* 3d ser., 7 (1950): 199–222.

22. Degler, "Slavery and the Genesis of American Race Prejudice," *Comparative Studies in Society and History* 2 (1959–1960): 492–96; Jordan, *White over Black: American Attitudes toward the Negro, 1550–1812* (Chapel Hill, N.C., 1968).

23. Menard, "Immigration and Opportunity: The Freedman in Early Colonial Maryland," in Thad W. Tate and David L. Ammerman, eds., *The Chesapeake*

in the Seventeenth Century: Essays on Anglo-American Society (Chapel Hill, N.C., 1979); Kulikoff, *Tobacco and Slaves*; Breen and Innes, *"Myne Owne Ground": Race and Freedom on Virginia's Eastern Shore, 1640–1676* (New York, 1980); Edmund Morgan, *American Slavery, American Freedom: The Ordeal of Colonial Virginia* (New York, 1975).

24. The phrase comes from Geertz, *The Interpretation of Cultures* (New York, 1973), 3; Wood, *Black Majority: Negroes in Colonial South Carolina from 1670 through the Stono Rebellion* (New York, 1974); Blassingame, *The Slave Community: Plantation Life in the Antebellum South* (New York, 1972); Isaac, *The Transformation of Virginia, 1740–1790* (Chapel Hill, N.C., 1982); Sobel, *The World They Made Together: Black and White Values in Eighteenth-Century Virginia* (Princeton, 1987).

25. Lemisch, "The American Revolution Seen from the Bottom Up," in Barton J. Bernstein, ed., *Towards a New Past: Dissenting Essays in American History* (New York, 1968), 3–45; Nash, "Social Change and the Growth of Prerevolutionary Urban Radicalism," in Young, ed., *The American Revolution: Explorations in the History of American Radicalism* (DeKalb, Ill., 1976), 3–36; Foner, "Tom Paine's Republic: Radical Ideology and Social Change," in Young, *American Revolution*, 187–232; Young, *The Democratic Republicans of New York: The Origins, 1763–1797* (Chapel Hill, N.C., 1967).

26. See, for example, Nash, *The Urban Crucible: Social Change, Political Consciousness, and the Origins of the American Revolution* (Cambridge, Mass., 1979).

27. See Young, *American Revolution*, esp. afterword, 447–62.

28. Murrin, "Anglicizing an American Colony: The Transformation of Provincial Massachusetts" (Ph.D. diss., Yale University, 1966).

29. Henretta, "Families and Farms: *Mentalité* in Pre-Industrial America," *William and Mary Quarterly*, 3d ser., 35 (1978): 3–32. The article rested in part on Henretta's synthesis of new scholarship in *The Evolution of American Society, 1700–1815: An Interdisciplinary Analysis* (Lexington, Mass., 1973). See also Michael Merrill, "Cash Is Good to Eat: Self-Sufficiency and Exchange in the Rural Economy of the United States," *Radical History Review* 3 (1977): 42–71.

30. Lemon, "Comment on James A. Henretta's 'Families and Farms: *Mentalité* in Pre-Industrial America,' with a Reply by James A. Henretta," *William and Mary Quarterly*, 3d ser., 37 (1980): 688–700. Henretta was reflecting on Lemon, *The Best Poor Man's Country: A Geographical Study of Early Southeastern Pennsylvania* (Baltimore, 1972).

31. Clark, *The Roots of Rural Capitalism: Western Massachusetts, 1780–1860* (Ithaca, N.Y., 1990); Brooke, *The Heart of the Commonwealth: Society and Political Culture in Worcester County, Massachusetts, 1713–1861* (New York, 1989); Pruitt, "Self-Sufficiency and the Agricultural Economy of Eighteenth-Century Massachusetts," *William and Mary Quarterly*, 3d ser., 41 (1984): 333–64; Rothenberg,

"The Emergence of a Capital Market in Rural Massachusetts, 1730–1838," *Journal of Economic History* 45 (1985): 781–808: and Rothenberg, "The Emergence of Farm Labor Markets and the Transformation of the Rural Economy: Massachusetts, 1750–1855," *Journal of Economic History* 48 (1988): 537–66; Innes, *Labor in a New Land: Economy and Society in Seventeenth-Century Springfield* (Princeton, 1983); Schweitzer, *Custom and Contract: Household, Government, and the Economy in Colonial Pennsylvania* (New York, 1987).

32. Vickers, *William and Mary Quarterly*, 3d. ser., 47 (1990): 3–29.

33. Derrida, "Structure, Sign, and Play in the Discourse of Human Sciences," in Richard Macksey and Eugenio Donato, eds., *The Languages of Criticism and the Sciences of Man* (Baltimore, 1970), 251.

34. Nash, *Red, White, and Black: The People of Early America,* 2d ed. (Englewood Cliffs, N.J., 1974), 1982.

35. Jennings, *The Invasion of America: Indians, Colonialism, and the Cant of Conquest* (Chapel Hill, N.C., 1975).

36. James Axtell, "The Ethnohistory of Early America: A Review Essay," *William and Mary Quarterly*, 3d ser., 35 (1978): 110–44; Sobel, *The World They Made Together.*

37. Axtell, *The Invasion Within: The Contest of Cultures in Colonial North America* (New York, 1985); Merrell, *The Indians' New World: Catawbas and Their Neighbors from European Contact through the Era of Removal* (Chapel Hill, N.C., 1989); Ronda, "'We Are Well As We Are': An Indian Critique of Seventeenth-Century Christian Missions," *William and Mary Quarterly*, 3d ser., 34 (1977): 66–82; Salisbury, *Manitou and Providence: Indians, Europeans, and the Making of New England, 1500–1643* (New York, 1982); Richter, "Cultural Brokers and Intercultural Politics: New York–Iroquois Relations, 1664–1701," *Journal of American History* 75 (1988): 40–67.

38. Schumpeter, "The Creative Response in Economic History," *Journal of Economic History* 7 (1947): 149–59; Pocock, *The Ancient Constitution and the Feudal Law: A Study of English Historical Thought in the Seventeenth Century* (Cambridge, 1957); Pocock, *Politics, Language, and Time: Essays on Political Thought and History* (New York, 1971); and Pocock, *The Machiavellian Moment: Florentine Political Thought and the Atlantic Republican Tradition* (Princeton, 1975).

39. Pocock, *Politics, Language, and Time*; Quentin Skinner, "Meaning and Understanding in the History of Ideas," *History and Theory* 8 (1969).

40. Bailyn, *The Ideological Origins of the American Revolution* (Cambridge, Mass., 1967).

41. The debate over republicanism can be followed in three articles: Robert E. Shalhope, "Toward a Republican Synthesis: The Emergence of an Understanding of Republicanism in American Historiography," *William and Mary*

Quarterly, 3d ser., 29 (1972): 49–80, Shalhope, "Republicanism and Early American Historiography," *William and Mary Quarterly*, 3d ser., 39 (1982): 334–56; and Daniel T. Rodgers, "Republicanism: The Career of a Concept," *Journal of American History* 79 (1992): 11–38.

42. Wood, *The Creation of the American Republic, 1776–1787* (Chapel Hill, N.C., 1969). Both explored the theoretical implications of their work in major articles—Bailyn, "The Central Themes of the American Revolution: An Interpretation," in Stephen G. Kurtz and James H. Hutson, eds., *Essays on the American Revolution* (Chapel Hill, N.C., 1973), 3–31, a publication of the papers from a 1969 Institute of Early American History and Culture conference; and Wood, "Rhetoric and Reality in the American Revolution," *William and Mary Quarterly*, 3d ser., 23 (1966): 3–32.

43. Robbins, *The Eighteenth-Century Commonwealthman: Studies in the Transmission, Development, and Circumstances of English Liberal Thought from the Restoration of Charles II until the War with the Thirteen Colonies* (Cambridge, 1962); Morgan and Morgan, *The Stamp Act Crisis: Prologue to Revolution* (Chapel Hill, N.C., 1953); Kenyon, "Republicanism and Radicalism in the American Revolution: An Old-Fashioned Interpretation," *William and Mary Quarterly*, 3d ser., 19 (1962): 153–82; Lokken, "The Concept of Democracy in Colonial Political Thought," *William and Mary Quarterly*, 3d ser., 16 (1959): 568–80; Pole, "Historians and the Problem of Early American Democracy," *American Historical Review* 67 (1962): 626–46.

44. Bailyn, "Central Themes of the American Revolution," 11; *Ideological Origins of the American Revolution*, 22ff., 56.

45. A special issue of *American Quarterly*, 37 (1985), explores the elaboration of the Republicanism theme in American history through the nineteenth century.

46. Richard R. Beeman, "Deference, Republicanism, and the Emergence of Popular Politics in Eighteenth-Century America," *William and Mary Quarterly*, 3d. ser., 49 (1992): 401–30; Isaac Kramnick, "The 'Great National Discussion': The Discourse of Politics in 1787," *William and Mary Quarterly*, 3d. ser., 45 (1988): 3–32; James T. Kloppenberg, "The Virtues of Liberalism: Christianity, Republicanism, and Ethics in Early American Political Discourse," *Journal of American History* 74 (1987): 9–33.

47. In the first issue of the third series of the *Quarterly*, the recently deceased Andrews is quoted as insisting that the colonial period was "something more than a time of incubation during which American ideals, principles, and faith were in embryo, or—to change the metaphor—something more than a seed-bed for the propagation of forms of government and habits of thought that would reach fruition only at a later period"; *William and Mary Quarterly*, 3d ser., 1 (1944): 28. See also Richard R. Johnson, "Charles McLean Andrews and the In-

vention of American Colonial History," *William and Mary Quarterly*, 3d ser., 43 (1986): 519–41.

48. Berger and Luckmann, *The Social Construction of Reality: A Treatise in the Sociology of Knowledge* (New York, 1966).

49. Miller, *The New England Mind: The Seventeenth Century* (New York, 1939); and Miller, *The New England Mind: From Colony to Province* (Cambridge, Mass., 1953); Kuhn, *The Structure of Scientific Revolutions* (Chicago, 1962). See also David A. Hollinger, "Perry Miller and Philosophical History," *History and Theory* 7 (1968): 189–202.

50. Hall, *The Faithful Shepherd: A History of the New England Ministry in the Seventeenth Century* (Chapel Hill, N.C., 1972); Foster, *Their Solitary Way: The Puritan Social Ethic in the First Century of Settlement in New England* (New Haven, Conn., 1971); Middlekauff, *The Mathers: Three Generations of Puritan Intellectuals, 1596–1728* (New York, 1971); McGiffert, "American Puritan Studies in the 1960s," *William and Mary Quarterly*, 3d ser., 27 (1970), 36–67; Hambrick-Stowe, *The Practice of Piety: Puritan Devotional Disciplines in Seventeenth-Century New England* (Chapel Hill, N.C., 1982); Fiering, "Will and Intellect in the New England Mind," *William and Mary Quarterly*, 3d ser., 29 (1972): 515–58; Pettit, *The Heart Prepared: Grace and Conversion in Puritan Spiritual Life* (New Haven, Conn., 1966); Stout, *The New England Soul: Preaching and Religious Culture in Colonial New England* (New York, 1986); Holifield, *The Covenant Sealed: The Development of Puritan Sacramental Theology in Old and New England, 1570–1720* (New Haven, Conn., 1974); and Cohen, *God's Caress: The Psychology of Puritan Religious Experience* (New Haven, Conn., 1986).

51. Hall, *Worlds of Wonder, Days of Judgment: Popular Religious Belief in Early New England* (New York, 1989); Butler, *Awash in a Sea of Faith: Christianizing the American People* (Cambridge, Mass., 1990); Bonomi, *Under the Cope of Heaven*.

52. Modernization theory lasted long enough to inspire one of the most interesting interpretations of early America in Richard D. Brown, *Modernization: The Transformation of American Life, 1600–1865* (New York, 1976).

3

THE AMERICAN HERITAGE:
THE HEIRS AND
THE DISINHERITED

Before there was a constitutional convention in Philadelphia in the summer of 1787, there was a little rebellion in western Massachusetts in the fall of 1786. So it is altogether fitting that the year before the celebration of the bicentennial of the Constitution there was a celebration of the bicentennial of Shays' Rebellion. Two decades of research on the lives of ordinary men and women have made more palpable what was involved in that series of court closings in Hampshire and Worcester counties in 1786 and how the military response to Daniel Shays' ragged platoons affected the lives of those who marched in opposition to the state's hard money policies. In these same twenty years we have also entered more sympathetically into the conceptual universe of the men—for the most part, members of the old colonial elite—who suppressed the Shaysites. I would like to draw from this research a few strands with which to weave a picture of the eighteenth-century world from which the U.S. Constitution came. It is clear in retrospect that the shared aspirations of some state leaders created "the more perfect union" of the United States and that the essential fragility of that union has been a dominant factor through most of America's history.

The characterization of the 1780s as a period of crisis comes from the writers of the Constitution themselves, most particularly the authors of the *Federalist Papers.* These men's alarm was real. James Madison felt it. George Washington expressed it, as did Edmund Randolph and Alexander Hamilton. But the leaders of Massachusetts did not, or did not until their draconian measures for repaying the state's revolutionary debt

This chapter first appeared as "The American Heritage: The Heirs and the Disinherited," *Journal of American History* 74 (December 1987). Copyright © Organization of American Historians. Reprinted with permission.

boomeranged in the Berkshires with Shays' Rebellion. By no means universal, this sense of crisis represented a particular response of specific leaders in some of the states. Among the gentry of Virginia it was marked. In fact almost all of the efforts to reform the Articles of the Confederation came from Virginia, starting with the casual gathering at Mount Vernon through the meeting the following year at Annapolis and on to the Philadelphia convention.[1] Shays' Rebellion (which came down to us as Shays' Rebellion through the writings of these same men) is important because it carried the consciousness of crisis to New England. Indeed it might be considered the functional equivalent of the Stamp Act in its consequent uniting of nationalists from Virginia and Massachusetts. Very quickly the court closings in western Massachusetts were converted into a symbolic event. The name, Shays' Rebellion, has carried a heavy load of ideological meaning ever since.[2]

The worries that the events in western Massachusetts provoked elsewhere had been gathering force since the end of the war. The state constitutions drafted in the wake of the Declaration of Independence concentrated governmental power in the legislatures. At the same time ordinary voters began electing ordinary men to represent them. Faced with mounting debt, both personal and public, these same legislators adopted policies favorable to their interests and the interests of their hard-pressed constituents. Because every state was faced with a revolutionary debt to pay off, taxes—their size, incidence, and form of payment—loomed large in postwar politics. Men with little money in coin, lots of personal debts, their capital tied up in land, wanted paper money issued with legal tender provisions for the payment of public and private debts. It was after all how the Revolution had been paid for through most of the fighting years. These same legislators often favored stay laws for the collection of taxes and statutes, which eased insolvency. Many of these measures had been passed during the Revolution when gentry leaders made concessions to popular demands. Afterward an increasingly articulate populace garnered enough votes to legislate without help from their social superiors. Controversies over land grants, electoral districts, and tax policies were resolved in favor of popular majorities in well over half the states. Hope that the upper houses of the legislatures would act as a check on the popular will had been swiftly dashed. Deference—the assumption that one's social superiors should exercise authority by virtue

of their eminence—disappeared with alarming rapidity. Viewed from the
perspective of established leaders, these developments were the stuff of
crisis. The emphasis that the authors of the *Federalist Papers* put on the
weakness of the Articles of Confederation has obscured the fact that it
was the strength and vigor of the state governments that had created a
sense of crisis among the old revolutionary elite.[3]

The democratization of the state governments was a sudden development—one with plenty of antecedents—but nonetheless sudden in its
full flowering during the immediate postwar years. There were constitutional implications in this shift of power. As the number of plain farmers
and representatives from the western parts of the states increased, majorities formed around the popular goals of increasing access to land, es-
tablishing land banks, and deferring the retirement of the public debt until personal financial security had been achieved. In pursuit of these
immediate goals, state legislatures more than once vaulted the limits of
their state constitutions. Their laws not only interfered with the value of
money and the certainty of private contracts, they also suggested a legislative indifference to constitutional restraints.

America in the 1780s had constitutions—a baker's dozen of them—
but not a culture of what I would call constitutionalism. As yet there had
developed no special aura around the notion of a constitution, despite the
great attention that French and English writers paid to America's phe-
nomenal outburst of constitution writing. In several states the constitutions themselves had become the focal point of controversy. Veneration
of constitutions did not figure prominently in public discourse, and campaigns to rewrite the state constitutions had begun with their ratification.
In Pennsylvania pro- and anticonstitutional parties dominated political
life until the Constitution was rewritten in 1790. Conflict held up the
signing of the Articles of Confederation until all of the fighting for
which the Confederation had been formed was over. This negligent attitude toward constitutions is surprising in view of the emphasis that was
placed on the British constitution and its part in guaranteeing liberty.
Many people worried about the cavalier attitude adopted by legislative
majorities toward the constitutions that empowered them. Thomas Jefferson, who hailed the blood shed in Shays' Rebellion as the natural manure for the tree of liberty, was far less tolerant of legislative supremacy
in Virginia. "The concentrating of the power of government in the same

hands," he wrote in his famous *Notes* is "precisely the definition of despotic government. . . . 173 despots would surely be as oppressive as one. . . . An elective despotism was not the government we fought for."[4]

It is all too tempting to think that the alarmed gentry leaders were reacting as an established interest group resisting pressure from below. And of course in a sense they were, but they were also responding as men thoroughly imbued with eighteenth-century ideas about civil order. It is surely one of the strengths of current ideological interpretations of the past that they promote an appreciation of the fact that men and women rarely do things out of a single motive. Rather they seem more impelled to act when a range of concerns prompts them. The ideological approach has also called into question the concept of simple self-interest unmediated by cultural perceptions of personal, private interests. Increasingly "self-interest" itself appears to be a cultural artifact, a theoretical triumph in the face of the natural profligacy of human motivation.

Recent efforts to understand why the popular state majorities of the revolutionary era created a sense of crisis have led to a remapping of the conceptual world of well-educated Anglo-Americans. Particularly salient in that universe was the British concept of balance as the metaphor for maintaining order among contending forces. In diplomacy it was the balance of power; in domestic relations it was the balanced constitution holding in check the opposing force of the few and the many. A conviction about natural inequality undergirds this social theory. Drawn from a variety of political treatises stretching forward from Aristotle through Machiavelli, Harrington and the century's own Montesquieu, this classical view of constitutionalism was tied to a rather ornate and not very American conception of the politician as the embodiment of male virtue (virtue came from the Greek word for man, *vir*). Citizens represented a special body of men, distinguished from women, children, and laborers by their social and economic independence.[5] The natural power lusts of human beings, high and the low, made civil society fragile, but the existence of two social groups available for checking each other supplied a solution entirely compatible with the gentlemen's notion of their special place in society. In much the same way as war makes gallantry possible so the frailty of civil order created a function for civic virtue. And just as those in love with military valor are rarely pacifists so those filled with admiration for balanced government had little faith in an undifferentiated citizenry. Values, it seems, rise above their practical origins.

Those classical republican concepts circulated more easily among gentle folk, for they were subjected to an early exposure to Greek and Roman texts. They also were more likely to accept the theory of natural inequality embedded in the classical gloss on the British constitution. Achieving stability by balancing the superior talents of the few against the numerical strength of the many meant, of course, that the few acted as the statesmen, judges, and generals who ran government while ordinary people existed politically to check any undue augmentation of elite power. Property played a key, if chameleon-like, role in this classical republican recipe for stability. It rooted men in their society and was supposed to liberate them for the practice of politics. Implicit in such an expectation is the view that property owners had an unproblematic hold on their property and could count on a stable living from it, a circumstance nicely captured in Edmund Burke's description of the English gentry's "unbought grace of uncontested ease." If truly independent financially, gentlemen could fulfill their destiny on the public stage while their ordinary human brethren fulfilled theirs in the less noble, private pursuits of planting and reaping, buying and selling, saving and investing. It's difficult to measure just how real the classical republican categories of thought appeared to the seaboard merchants, tidewater planters, and prosperous farmers who composed the American elite. Nonetheless, their public statements are filled with republican themes: order is fragile; power lusts fill all men; virtue is imperiled by ambition and desire; only those immune from the pressures of everyday want can be trusted with responsibility.

Developments since the emergence of an integrated European trade had made economic life more ebullient than placid and nowhere more so than in the North American colonies.[6] Property rooted men in their society until they decided to move. Deriving an income from that property required constant attention to cues about price and preferences in distant markets. American participation in the Atlantic trade world undermined the economic stability on which classical republican political ideals rested. The implications of this system had not yet been fully elaborated in intellectual formulations. Earlier assumptions remained embedded in sensibilities, causing the James Madisons and George Washingtons of the day to look with real concern on the legislative manipulation of currency and the obvious self-interest of debtor-made laws. The state constitutions that had been written in the wake of the Declaration of Independence had not elicited reverence, thus rendering uncertain their explicit limitations on the exercise of government power. Viewed through classical republican prisms, this was not new-modeled democracy but old-foreshadowed anarchy. Unbalanced state constitutions were plunging society back into the cyclical turbulence predicted for those benighted people who had not learned from the past. Despite their experience with the dynamic changes of the eighteenth century, many of America's revolutionary elite still thought in terms of decline and degeneration. Comfortable with their long-established use of power in a status-structured society, they found the similar use of power in the interest of an undifferentiated people unsettling. And when they gave expression to these unsettled feelings, they did so in the language of classical republicanism pointing to unbalanced constitutions, the uncertainty of property, and the weakness of government at the center.

The presuppositions and prejudices of eighteenth-century Americans ordered their reality, but they were not orderly. American society at the end of the eighteenth century was undergoing dramatic change, but no coherent social theory about change existed. More and more the important arena for social action came to be the area of free bargaining and voluntary association rather than the polity presumed to exist in classical thought. Hence, inherited ways of thinking lost their material base. Institutions created to secure old goals of solidarity and persistence slowly became irrelevant; others took on new significance. The protection of property in a world predicated on the economic stasis of classical republicanism was meant to secure the virtue of the rulers and the rule of the virtuous. The protection of property rights in an economy of enhanced productivity and greater risk-taking guaranteed the gains of successful market participants.

Looking at the classical republican worldview as an orientation to reality, we can imagine that the Founding Fathers' reaction to social change involved enthusiasm and fear, selective blindness and anticipatory appreciation. With sensibilities rooted in the past and with information formulated from experience, the men and women of the late eighteenth century were forced to live with constant social change and with divided intellectual loyalties. Historians have drawn on the sociology of knowledge and cultural anthropology to reconstruct how structured consciousness influences social action. Their findings in turn have contributed to a reassessment of the connections between belief and behavior. Seeking usable generalizations, social scientists have written of systems of thought and symbolic meaning. A more accurate metaphor for what historians have found would be a patchwork of thought. The elements of an ideology are joined together like a quilt, their design coming from selection and repetition, not logic.[7] Thus the elements of classical republicanism found in eighteenth-century writings attest to the persistence of ideas no longer capable of illuminating reality.

The fifty-five delegates who gathered in the State House at Philadelphia may have had their normative vision formed in the matrix of classical republican ideals, but they achieved their place in the constitutional convention because their experience had made them highly pragmatic leaders with a continental outlook. They knew well the character of ordinary American voters and how that character limited their choices. Had they been able to ensure the preponderating influence of gentlemen in the upper house, they could have used bicameralism as a check on popular power. Without deferential social habits, the distinction between the few and the many lost its political function. Faced with these intractable realities, the "Demi-Gods" meeting in Philadelphia came up with a liberal solution to their classical republican problem of balance. Without clearly demarked social groups to check each other's usurpations of power, the Constitution drafters limited the power of both state and federal legislatures. They created a national government where none had existed but nonetheless departed from British precepts and classical republican formulas by specifying the legislature's power. To maintain the constitutional limits on power they relied on the self-interest of individual officeholders to preserve the boundaries among the legislative, executive, and judicial branches of government. "Ambition must be made to counteract ambition," Madison wrote in the *Federalist Papers*, no. 51, "The interests of the man must be connected with the constitutional rights of the place."[8]

Self-interest was accepted as a functional equivalent to civic virtue, but at the same time the scope of government, particularly the power of state government to legislate in economic matters, was severely limited.

If the old balance of the few and the many acting in the interests of the whole could not be reestablished, a new balance of opposing interests would not be asked to do as much. Article 1, Section 10 of the Constitution indicates just how much was taken away from the states. Listed there are the disallowed powers that had wreaked such havoc in postrevolutionary politics: the power to coin money, emit bills of credit, make anything but gold and silver coin legal tender, pass laws impairing the obligation of contracts, or lay any import or export duties. The Constitution created a national government to replace a confederation of sovereign states, but it limited the power of that national government as well through the enumeration of powers. At both levels of the new federalism the Constitution provided for a more limited government, especially in the economic realm. Thomas Paine had popularized a novel distinction between society and government in the opening lines of *Common Sense.* "Society," he wrote, "is produced by our wants, and government by our wickedness; the former promotes our happiness positively by uniting our affections, the latter negatively by restraining our vices."[9] The U.S. Constitution institutionalized that division by restricting the ambit of legislation as it simultaneously enlarged the constitutionally protected domain of free association. Thus the liberalism of the Constitution inheres less in the unleashing of interest group politics than in the enlargement of the social sphere, newly conceived as what Jefferson called "the empire of liberty."

The Constitution closed the door on simple majoritarian government in the United States. Popular majorities animated by what people wanted to do at a particular moment would be forever constrained. The Constitution created a fundamental law and that law severely restricted the range of government power. That same founding document made it extraordinarily difficult to change the distribution of power. Despite the celebration of popular sovereignty in America, the sovereign people were restrained once the Constitution was ratified. Perhaps nothing in the Constitution has worked more against democracy than the amendment process. One-quarter of the states plus one can always veto the affirmed choice of three-quarters of the states minus one. If the denying states were not very populous, perhaps a tenth of the citizenry could block the will of the remaining nine-tenths. In place of a politics of active involvement, the Constitution provided for the distant administration of national law. And even this centripetal force was minimized when Jefferson dismantled the Federalist program after his election.

What was left for nationalist sentiment to feed on was an abstract union embodied in a written Constitution. The culture of constitutionalism forthwith took the place of a powerful central government as the nation's unifier. Where the state constitutions remained political documents to be repeatedly rewritten and amended, the U.S. Constitution was elevated to a revered status almost immediately after its passage. The still unreconciled and profound political differences among the revolutionary elite found an outlet in party building in the 1790s while expressions of fidelity to the Constitution provided the ideological glue for the loosely bound United States in the antebellum period. With this promising material, John Marshall created a judicial tradition that separated law from politics and made of the Constitution an effective arbiter of democratic will. Whereas classical republicanism had promoted a fear of power and a respect for the liberty-securing promise of civil society, American ideology increasingly produced a disparagement of government and a reverence for the Constitution that protected the domain of natural liberty from the now suspect powers of government.[10]

It is hard to believe that there was ever a possibility of a fully participatory democracy in the United States. Or perhaps more accurately, it appears unlikely to most scholars that such a participatory democracy would have decisively changed the course of national development once the crucial connections among capital, technology, and resources was made in the nineteenth century. Such an attitude draws strength from a historiographical tradition that overdetermines the outcome of industrial capitalism. Whether from a Marxist or a liberal perspective, the transformative force of industrialization has been treated as inevitable, entailing a seemingly inexorable succession of structural changes sweeping through the purposive realm of politics. Empirically, the similarity today of capitalist economies in Western Europe and the United States bolsters the predisposition we already have to minimize the influence that different political institutions might have exercised. Against this view, I would argue that every difference makes a difference. Unlike eighteenth-century Europe, the United States had the material for democratic politics in 1787. A large proportion of adult white men held land, voted, and engaged in political debates on issues elsewhere considered the province of officials. Foreign visitors in the eighteenth century invariably commented on the vitality of public discussion and on the political confidence of ordinary men. Had the states been left with the economic powers they had before the ratification of the U.S. Constitution, the momentum of popular politics would not have been checked. Never having lost the normal scope of legislative power, the states could more easily have maintained the traditional connection between government and social responsibility, exercising in the economic realm a responsibility that they continued to exercise in matters of morals when they legislated intrusively on drinking habits, marriage choices, sexual practices, race relations, and a whole range of other personal liberties that have received constitutional protection only in the past few decades. Without constitutional protection, it seems unlikely that private property rights would ever have achieved their rhetorical status as sacred. This is not to suggest that the majority of Americans disliked the market economy or that commercial expansion would not have taken place. People acting in their capacity as citizens with the power of the state at their collective disposal could have had a larger part in making decisions. The social and the economic would not have been constitutionally divided, and ordinary men in America could have shaped the course of commerce as part of government and not simply as individual buyers and sellers.

Creating a national government was an open-ended goal. We speak of strengthening the government in 1787 as though there was only one way to do it and hence justify the particular provisions of the Constitution on the grounds that the national union needed strengthening. There were alternatives to the one issuing from Philadelphia. The dismay of Antifederalists at the specific provisions of the Constitution arose as much as anything from their regret at the roads not taken. Much less coherent in their opposition than the Federalists, they nonetheless articulated a defense of democracy that serves to remind us of a very important alternative abandoned. A more sympathetic reading of Antifederalist polemics restores that sense of possibilities, which has been deadened by two centuries of veneration for the Constitution; it also revives for our consideration their skepticism about a contemporary crisis in the sovereign states. The "crisis" urged on the public by the Federalists and frequently believed in since did not alarm the men who opposed the Philadelphia draft constitution. They insisted that Americans lived in peace and tranquility, secure enough to consider reform in a leisurely manner. They did not share the same apprehensions that popular politics would degenerate into majority tyranny, or, more accurately, they considered the tensions between liberty and equality supportable. No less concerned than the Federalists with the expanding horizons of self-improvement held out by commercial progress, the Antifederalists did not posit a fundamental incompatibility between legislative activism and private property rights. Hence they did not see the necessity of resolving the tension between the two in favor of the economic freedoms of the individual.[11]

Nothing weakens a position so much as losing. If this is generally the case, it is a fortiori on an issue of such fundamental importance as the ratification of a constitution. The opinions of the Antifederalists have been trapped in the ambergris of one political decision. Their views have not, like those of the Federalists, lived on to be incorporated with the history of their success. Although it seems a mistake to treat the Antifederalists as more than a disparate group connected by one shared choice, their writings in 1787 and 1788 serve as powerful reminders that other constitutions could have been written. Like the history of science, the history of the U.S. Constitution has been largely written as the history of its progress.

Martin Diamond once told his students that the history of the United States could be told as the creation of an American heritage and the fight among the heirs. He thus wittily encapsulated a familiar view in the 1950s: that the two major political parties divided the moral capital of the United States. More specifically they had divvied up equality and liberty between them. At a time when the two-party system was hardly less awe-inspiring to Americans than the Constitution, it was comforting to think of each political party drawing on a different trust fund. I am tempted to rewrite Diamond's line and say that the history of American constitutionalism can now be told as the creation of the American heritage and the fight between the heirs and the disinherited. It is fascinating to think of the events of our own time, which have made possible this revision. We can catalog the predisposing factors: the civil rights campaign, the interest in ethnicity, and the women's movement. It speaks as well to a quiet revolution in the American professoriate. The GI Bill introduced working-class men and women—many of them second- and third-generation immigrants—to college education, and the subsequent expansion in higher education opened up university jobs to them a few years later. No longer the preserve of upper-middle-class WASP men, history faculties began to reflect the ethnic and racial diversity in the nation at large. The computer facilitated the social historians' reconstruction of the lives of ordinary Americans through the quantitative analysis of vital records. All of these developments have influenced the lines of inquiry pursued by historians who entered the profession in the 1960s. Those historians came from different backgrounds, and they brought questions that bore a family resemblance to those asked by their patrician predecessors: Where are my forebears in the American past, and what was their place in that past?

The idea of looking at the history of the Constitution as a fight between the heirs and the disinherited opens up some interesting perspectives. First, because there was an American heritage—a national trust fund of political ideals—there were the roles of heirs and disinherited to be played out. I think that this explains the loyalty of the disinherited to the Constitution and why the Constitution has been a bastion for the elite as well as a vehicle for reform. Reformers have rarely turned against the Constitution—William Lloyd Garrison's burning of the document is an inflammatory exception—because the Constitution has represented a standard of justice to be held up to those with power. Reformers have actually drawn from two ideological fonts: that of inalienable rights articulated in the Declaration of Independence and the Bill of Rights and that of fundamental law determining the proper distribution of power embodied in the Constitution. The merging of these two sources of meaning has intensified the constitutionalism of most American reform groups. Had the Constitution been the sole womb of political values in America, its conservative bias would have become more apparent. As it is, equality and liberty, justice and freedom, have lived together for so long in our imagination that we think of them as legally married, even well matched. The promiscuous blending of these traditions accounts as well for the discomfort felt when Charles Beard disentangled the two by interpreting the Constitution as a Thermidorian response to the revolutionary ideals of the Declaration of Independence.[12] That Beard's interpretation held sway for but a generation in the two hundred years of writing on the Constitution indicates the powerful appeal of a single American heritage.[13]

The Constitution has also provided a civilized arena for power struggles framed by the concept of civil rights. The Bill of Rights—to return to my metaphoric fight—created a codicil to the Founders' will, decisively shaping the character of reform in America. The existence of this particular arena for conflict suggests why a Thurgood Marshall or a Catherine MacKinnon goes to law school; it also helps explain the coolness some radicals feel for the critical legal studies movement. Fundamental law may be a fundamentally flawed concept, but its resonance with the heirs has created a hostage for the disinherited. And both have shared in the dismissive attitude toward government implicit in Paine's distinction between society and government. The "people's power" evoked by protesters in the 1960s found little support in the nation at large, no doubt because Americans are used to thinking of majority will as a threat, against which the Constitution is their sheet anchor.

Despite the reformers' use of the Constitution, we should not be fooled into thinking that the heirs and the disinherited have had an equal payout from the inheritance. Probate judges, to continue my metaphor, have usually found for the heirs. The existence of a constitutional standard of justice may have mobilized a succession of reform groups, but it has been even more effective in protecting those who benefit directly from its dispensations. The Constitution has structured power in America, as well as the bad faith of the powerful. The mystification of fundamental law has enabled the beneficiaries to pose as the passive conservers of tradition. New England leaders did not shed their belief in the superiority of the few. They continued to worry about what would maintain order in a society lacking an established church, an attachment to place, and the uncontested leadership of men of merit. Into that void they poured an avalanche of words, the most powerful of which turned out to be the ones that created a legal science for interpreting the Constitution. Once their jurisprudential nationalism triumphed with the victorious Union Army, judges and lawyers began emphasizing the Constitution's organic connection to the American experience as distinguished from its origins in a contract of states.[14] Thus mystified, the Constitution was ratcheted up another notch above the level of participatory, democratic politics.

The very inequality of the opposing sides using the Constitution—those defending a conservative, sometimes literal reading and those articulating a more radical, underlying meaning—accounts for the emphasis on strategy we find in the labor and civil rights movements. Had there not been a fundamental law set above majoritarian politics, many of the goals of reforming groups could have been achieved through the direct use of legislative power. Instead, reform movements in America have often taken on the character of military tactics in a fixed terrain.[15] There has been no similar civil rights movement in Great Britain, not because there are no civil rights there but because Parliament has full legislative power. British reformers have availed themselves of that power. In a single vote Parliament abolished slavery in the British Empire. Nowhere in the government of the United States was there ever lodged the power to abolish slavery. As the custodians of rights, the handful of interpreters of the Constitution have exercised far more power than the electorate.

The American heritage and the fight between the heirs and the disinherited tells only part of the story. An equally important reality in the history of America is the fact that the Constitution entered a culture already fully fitted out with symbolic systems and sacred texts. References to the newness of the nation should not obscure the age of the thirteen societies that comprised the United States. The most important source of meaning for Americans, of course, was the Bible. From eighteen centuries of biblical interpretations came Calvinism, Arminianism, Unitarianism, evangelicalism, antinomianism, and millenarianism—Christian traditions that were rich with conceptual imagery, potent symbols, and prescriptive models for behavior. The Bible as it was variously interpreted in America's proliferating denominations provided the basis for justifying the inferiority of women, explaining the differences among the races, and structuring familial relations, not to mention conveying the sexual taboos of western Christendom. The culture of constitutionalism that emerged within the first fifty years after ratification had to be reconciled with these already established traditions, a process fraught with ambiguities, if not outright contradictions.[16]

It has always been in the interest of the heirs to blend constitutional interpretations with those of the common law and of the Bible, just as it has usually been in the interest of the disinherited to point out the contradictions between the equality in natural rights philosophy and the acceptance of older hierarchies. For many of the heirs, the rights discourse was an irritating intrusion into a settled, biblically ordained order. Thomas Huxley's remark that there was "no damned nonsense about rights in the Bible" nicely captures this point of view. Hardly less pregnant with meaning than the Bible for eighteenth-century Americans was the common law whose commanding presence imposed the necessity of integration with the newly minted political arrangements of the Constitution. Like the Bible, the common law provided little support for natural rights philosophy. For no Americans was this more important than the industrial workers whose "rights" were most often discussed under the common law's rules for masters and servants. Against the prescriptive rights of employers, workers in the emerging industrial economy appealed alternately to their variant of republicanism and to individual rights.[17]

The radical potential offered after 1787 was the opportunity to rethink the judicial imperatives of the Bible and the common law and perhaps replace them with legislation, a program embraced by the codifiers of the early nineteenth century. The prescriptive hierarchy of men over women, however, worked against the cooperation of black men and disenfranchised women. Having earlier sought the vote as a fundamental right, women, after the ratifications of the Thirteenth Amendment, constructed arguments around their peculiar situation. "This shift from arguments based on the common humanity of men and women," as Ellen DuBois has written, "to arguments based on fundamental differences of the sexes—has its parallel in virtually every feminist epoch."[18] Whether "disinherited" men—blacks, workers—have been opportunistic or sexist in dissociating their cause from that of women, the chilling effect has been the same. Similarly the common law protected the free market from efforts of workers in the late nineteenth century to achieve collective goals. With the rejection after the Civil War of the concept of the Constitution as a compact of states, constitutionalism merged with historicism to form the American variant of immanent values unfolding in space and time. Here again the haze of veneration that obscures the original reception of the Constitution hides as well the conceptual problems involved in integrating the Constitution into the didactic traditions of eighteenth-century America.

Against the philosophical depiction of the Constitution as a disembodied ideal working itself out in history, Beard launched his interpretation of the Constitution. "Man, as a political animal acting upon political, as distinguished from more vital and powerful motives," Beard wrote, "is the most unsubstantial of all abstractions."[19] In order to free his generation from its veneration of the Constitution, Beard ironically rejected the validity of political motives. Attempting to recapture the revolutionary potential of 1776 for the working classes of 1913, Beard demystified the Constitution by reducing the purposes in the constitutional movement to the pecuniary motives of the Founding Fathers. Reading the *Federalist*, no. 10 as a gloss on economic liberalism, he implicitly denied that politics could rise above individual self-interest. John Diggins has recently made a case for Beard's engagement with the issue of authority created by the Constitution's limitations on sovereignty.[20] But Beard brought the Founding Fathers down from their pedestals by ridiculing the community of interests that informed their efforts. He thus began a historiographical tradition that construed human motivation through a radical individualism that did not exist in 1787. The drafters of the Constitution were cultural innovators when they relied on self-interested individualism to provide the checks and balances once supplied by well-defined social classes. The historians of republicanism who in recent years have revised our understanding of the framing of the Constitution have made it possible to measure just how dramatic a cultural change the liberal elements in the Constitution effected. They have also discovered in the American past a form of community that holds out the promise of revitalizing contemporary politics.[21] Two hundred years later, it is the dysfunctional aspect of relying on self-interest that is apparent.

The Constitution removed a broad range of legislative powers in the economic domain from the state legislatures where popular majorities most effectively wielded power. The subsequent division between law and politics, elaborated by Marshall and Story, gave to the Constitution a moral stature denied the political process. Fundamental law became hypostasized as a source of justice removed from the workaday world of partisan elections and legislative bargaining. Majority will in action lost the normative standing accorded the people as the onetime ratifiers of the Constitution. Over time a culture of constitutionalism emerged that blended the Constitution with the higher law tradition associated with the common law. Both conservatives and reformers—the heirs and the disinherited—contributed to the veneration of the Constitution. By the end of the nineteenth century, the Constitution had become the symbolic protector of Americans' natural rights. And that tradition merged with larger themes of Western civilization: belief in an essential human nature and in objective standards of justice.[22]

Thomas Haskell outlines the perils that those concepts face in the intellectual milieu of the late twentieth century. The question that he poses—why the paradoxical persistence of rights talk in an age of interpretation—joins the history of the American Constitution to the contemporary crisis of Western metaphysics. The pivot for Haskell's argument is Nietzsche's query, What is the difference between "I want x" and "I have a right to x." By asking that, Nietzsche challenged the credibility of the natural law tradition, which assigned to human reason the capacity to establish objective truths that could be used to distinguish between power and right. Developments in almost all disciplines since Nietzsche's time have intensified his radical skepticism. Belief in reason operating independently of the historically situated reasoner has been under attack for over a century. Anthropological investigations of the multifarious human cultures on the globe have called into question Western civilization's claim to speak for the entire human race. At the same time, analyses of what is involved in reading and writing, speaking and hearing have transformed language into a medium for creating, rather than for discovering, reality. To paraphrase Haskell, the paradoxical coexistence in recent American culture of statements implying objectivity and a deep skepticism about the theoretical possibility of achieving such objectivity that makes contemporary moral discourse incoherent. Even though our new appreciation of culture suggests that conventions and not revelations rule our concepts of justice, the persistence of rights talk, he observes, implies an aspiration to base our moral arguments on appeals to reason. Haskell does not agree with Nietzsche that rights claims sink or swim with the Western flagship of objective knowledge. The recognition that reason does not exist independently of time and place does not deny its existence within time and place. Haskell asserts that rights can be viewed as conventions, vital components of America's constitutional culture, exportable as ideals worthy of persuasive talk. Quoting John Rawls, Haskell concurs that what justifies a conception of justice is not an antecedent intellectual order, but rather congruence to a deeper understanding of ourselves.[23]

A deeper understanding of ourselves can lead to a heightened awareness of the contradictions that rage within and without. That we can levitate ourselves intellectually outside our cultural predispositions long enough to recognize their existence does not liberate us from their hold. The national commitment to a constitutional order with a natural rights foundation was added on to a culture that was profoundly racist and sexist. That contradiction has exercised a dynamic power for two centuries. Reformers have repeatedly sought to expose it; conservatives have evoked a concept of nature that restored the hierarchy once maintained by tradition. The crisis of natural rights discourse in the age of interpretation is not confined to the revelation that fundamental law has no secure foundation in objective knowledge. It also resides in the specific assertions of Western philosophy, particularly its creation of human culture in its own image. Westerners have built their science as well as their institutions on specific propositions about human nature that our expanded knowledge of other societies denies. As Jacques Derrida has noted, we are living through "a de-centering of European culture" when Western metaphysics is being "driven from its locus and forced to stop considering itself as the culture of reference."[24] Yet the very desire to ground belief in objective knowledge and the accompanying despair that it cannot be done suggest that renunciation of the center comes hard. The more troubling question may well be whether or not we can maintain our cultural center of gravity unweighted by belief in the universality of the characteristics of the autonomous Western man.

Anthropological studies of culture offer a powerful challenge to the belief in the universality of Western norms. But more than intellectual insight is involved. It will require an unprecedented act of humility for defenders of Western civilization to accept the fact that their view of nature is merely a convention. Mere convention cannot prove that constitutions are superior to customs, science to myth, individualism to corporatism, progress to stasis, work to play, experimentation to contemplation, and law to politics. Exploring these preferences as conventions leads away from universal propositions toward particular mores. To convince others involves leveling appeals to experience and the abandonment of didactic demonstrations of proof. An appreciation for cultural differences offers a powerful solvent to Western hubris, and therein lies hope—a hope especially welcome to those who have felt the sting of universalist assumptions. But the decentering of which Derrida speaks affects the heirs and the disinherited very differently. For the heirs of the American heritage, an elegiac mood prevails; the loss of the possibility of certainty is grave. For the disinherited there is the possibility of liberation from a language of rights accompanied by a practice of denial. For both, doctrine will have to yield to explanation. A rich opportunity beckons, that of looking at the history of the Constitution as the record of people contending about power, identity, and justice.

NOTES

1. H. James Henderson, "The Structure of Politics in the Continental Congress," in *Essays on the American Revolution*, ed. Stephen G. Kurtz and James H. Hutson (Chapel Hill, N.C.), 190–92.

2. Van Beck Hall, *Politics without Parties: Massachusetts, 1780–1792* (Pittsburgh, 1972), 256. David P. Szatmary, *Shays' Rebellion: The Making of an Agrarian Insurrection* (Amherst, Mass., 1980).

3. Jackson Turner Main, *Political Parties before the Constitution* (Chapel Hill, N.C., 1973); and Merrill Jensen, *The New Nation* (New York, 1950).

4. Thomas Jefferson, *Notes on the State of Virginia*, ed. William Peden (Chapel Hill, N.C., 1955), 120.

5. Gordon S. Wood, *The Creation of the American Republic, 1776–1787* (Chapel Hill, N.C., 1969); and J. G. A. Pocock, *The Machiavellian Moment: Florentine Political Thought and the Atlantic Republican Tradition* (Princeton, 1975).

6. Marc Egnal and Joseph A. Ernst, "An Economic Interpretation of the American Revolution," *William and Mary Quarterly* 29 (January 1972); and John J. McCusker and Russell R. Menard, *The Economy of British America* (Chapel Hill, N.C., 1985).

7. Peter L. Berger and Thomas Luckmann, *The Social Construction of Reality: A Treatise in the Sociology of Knowledge* (New York, 1966).

8. James Madison et al., *The Federalist Papers* (New York, 1937), 337.

9. Thomas Paine, *Common Sense,* ed. Isaac Kramnick (New York, 1976), 65.

10. Jennifer Nedelsky, "Confining Democratic Politics: Anti-Federalists, Federalists, and the Constitution," *Harvard Law Review* 96 (1982), especially 358–60. As R. Kent Newmyer detailed in "Harvard Law School, New England Legal Culture, and the Antebellum Origins of American Jurisprudence," *Journal of*

American History 74 (December 1987), even Marshall's substantial work was insufficient to impose order on the Constitution's many judicial interpreters in the first three decades of the nineteenth century.

11. Herbert Storing, *What the Anti-Federalists Were For: The Political Thought of the Opponents of the Constitution* (Chicago, 1981); and Nedelsky, "Confining Democratic Politics."

12. Charles A. Beard, *An Economic Interpretation of the Constitution of the United States* (New York, 1913).

13. Morton Keller, "Politics, Government, and the Constitution," *Journal of American History* 74 (December 1987).

14. Newmyer, "Harvard Law School."

15. Eric Foner, "Rights and the Constitution in Black Life during the Civil War and Reconstruction," *Journal of American History* 74 (December 1987); Ellen DuBois, "Girls Just Want to Have Rights: Equal Rights, Woman Suffrage and the U.S. Constitution, 1820–1875," *Journal of American History* 74 (December 1987); and Leon Fink, "Labor, Liberty and the Law: Trade Unionism and the Problem of Collective Actions within the American Constitutional Order," *Journal of American History* 74 (December 1987).

16. Martha Minow, "We, the Family: Constitutional Rights and American Families," *Journal of American History* 74 (December 1987).

17. Fink, "Labor, Liberty and the Law"; and Staughton Lynd, "The Genesis of the Idea of a Community Right to Industrial Property in Youngstown and Pittsburgh, 1977–86," *Journal of American History* 74 (December 1987).

18. DuBois, "Girls Just Want to Have Rights."

19. Max Lerner, "The Constitution and Court as Symbols," *Yale Law Journal* 46 (June 1937), 32; and Frank Michelman, "The Supreme Court; 1985 Term: Forward: Traces of Self-Government," *Harvard Law Review,* November 1986.

20. John P. Diggins, "Power and Authority in American History: The Case of Charles A. Beard and His Critics," *American Historical Review* 86 (October 1981): 701–30.

21. Wood, *Creation of the American Republic.*

22. Thomas L. Haskell, "The Curious Persistence of Rights Talk in the 'Age of Interpretation,'" *Journal of American History* 74 (December 1987).

23. Haskell, "Curious Persistence."

24. Jacques Derrida, "Structure, Sign and Play in the Discourse of the Human Science," in *The Languages of Criticism and the Sciences of Man,* ed. Richard Macksey and Eugenia Donato (New York, 1970), 251.

4

RECOVERING AMERICA'S HISTORIC DIVERSITY: BEYOND EXCEPTIONALISM

Before America became a nation it was a phenomenon. In the reform-minded salons of Paris, at commemorative gatherings of London nonconformists, among emergent working-class radicals, the struggle for independence undertaken by thirteen of Britain's North American colonies was given ideological shape and weight and infused with magnetic force. "They are the hope of the human race, they may well become its model," Anne Robert Turgot told Richard Price. Denis Diderot proclaimed the newly founded United States an asylum from fanaticism and tyranny "for all the peoples of Europe." Thomas Jefferson's young secretary, William Short, who remained in Paris after Jefferson returned home to become secretary of state, elaborated on this asylum theme when he compared Americans to a group of prisoners who have broken out of "a common goal" and are being watched by their fellow inmates with "an anxious eye" to see if escape is possible. Summarizing these European reactions, the French historian Bernard Faye concluded, "Not a book on America was printed between 1775 and 1790 but ended with a sort of homily," which prompted another historian, Durand Echeverria, to depict Europeans creating for themselves a "Mirage in the West."[1] We could call this America an Enlightenment version—or perversion—of Pandora's box, filled with all the social cravings from a restless European spirit that once freed were scattered to the four winds leaving behind only doubt.

From these sophisticated reflections about a colonial rebellion 3,000 miles away came American exceptionalism, a concept that began in

This chapter first appeared as "Recovering America's Historic Diversity: Beyond Exceptionalism," *Journal of American History* 79 (September 1992). Copyright © Organization of American Historians. Reprinted with permission.

high-spirited conversations and ended as an uncontested assumption structuring the political consciousness of the American people. Exceptional does not mean different. All nations are different; and almost all national sentiments exploit those differences. Exceptionalism does more; it projects onto a nation—in this case a cluster of newly independent states—qualities that are envied because they suggest deliverance from a common lot. There are no exceptions without well-understood generalizations or norms in contrast to which the exceptional commands attention. The United States became a political prodigy in reference to a consensus shared by Continental philosophes, English Dissenters, and radical pamphleteers. These Europeans celebrated American anomalies because they proved that reform was possible, that, to use Short's metaphor, the escaping prisoners would sustain the hopes of those left behind. But even if European draftsmen sketched the lineaments of this exceptional new nation, the picture found its enduring appeal in the United States because it offered eighteenth-century Americans a collective identity before they had any other basis for spiritual unity. Pushed into prominence in the contentious politics of the 1790s, exceptionalism formed the core concept of popular political rhetoric. Turgot's "hope of the human race" was then transmogrified into a peculiar destiny; what had been contingent and adventitious in the colonial past acquired purpose and momentum. A grand narrative was adumbrated. Those events that had preceded the Declaration of Independence were reinterpreted as preparations of it. The year 1776 marked both a culmination and a beginning.

Exceptionalism, in this analysis, is America's peculiar form of Eurocentrism. In the nation's critical first decades, it provided a way to explain the U.S. connection to Europe in a story about its geographic and political disconnection. But today exceptionalism raises formidable obstacles to appreciating America's original and authentic diversity. What I have designated as our peculiar form of Eurocentrism created a national identity for the revolutionary generation, and at the same time that identity foreclosed other ways of interpreting the meaning of the United States. It is to that foreclosure two centuries ago that we should now look in order to diagnose our present discomfort with calls for a multicultural understanding of America. During the past quarter century historical scholarship has begun to free our imagination from the impress of that venerable tale about a singular national destiny. The rich implications of this new work invite us to move beyond the polemics of multicultural-ism to its rewarding possibilities. In order to recover America's historical diversity, we will need to examine the intellectual wraps that have hid-den it from us.

America, in the minds of its attentive European observers of the eighteenth century, was exceptional because its healthy, young, hard-working population had won a revolutionary prize of an empty conti-nent on which to settle its freeborn progeny. America was exceptional because the familiar predators of ordinary folk—the extorting tax col-lector, the overbearing nobleman, the persecuting priest, the extravagant ruler—had failed to make the voyage across the Atlantic. Natural abun-dance, inhabitants schooled in tolerance, historic exemption from Old World social evils—these were the materials with which the European reform imagination worked to create the exceptional United States.

Elisabeth d'Houdetot expressed American exceptionalism with fine Gallic clarity in a letter to Jefferson. Writing in 1790 when the violent career of the French Revolution had barely begun, she noted that "the characteristic difference between your revolution and ours is that having nothing to destroy, you had nothing to injure, and labouring for a peo-ple, few in number, incorrupted, and extended over a large tract of coun-try, you have avoided all the inconvenience of a situation, contrary in every respect. Every step in your revolution was perhaps the effect of virtue, while ours are often faults, and sometimes crimes."[2] Here is a de-piction of American exceptionalism in its pristine form.

But think what is missing from this rather patronizing description of America's "contrary situation." There is no hint of the daily, perfunc-tory brutality of a slave institution that incorporated mandatory physical abuse of men, women, and children into the laws of a majority of the newly united states. Nor did awareness of the systematic ejection and ex-termination of the indigenous population mar Madame d'Houdetot's benign depiction of "a people, few in number, incorrupted, and extended over a large tract of country." We might explain her failure to discuss these acts of oppression from a nation dedicated to liberty and equality on the grounds that acquaintances rarely take the occasion of a friendly letter to abrade each other's sensibilities. But I think these lacunae signify more than politeness. Madame d'Houdetot's conceptual optic nerve could not pick up the colors of black and red because already Europeans had learned to make the other invisible. And the citizens of the United States followed their lead. Accepting a role in the new script about an age of revolutions, many Americans extended the category of invisible others to those who failed to play their part in the high drama of progress. Increasingly white Americans came to view the founding of a free and equal people as their calling in the world and as they did so their collective remembrance of the diverse purposes animating colonial settlements atrophied. Necessity mothered this ideological invention because Americans in 1776 had to create the sense of nationhood that other countries inherited. U.S. nationhood—its juridical standing—preceded the formation of a national ideology and this peculiar inversion of sentiment and status led to a quest for national identity. Americans had not only not lived long in their land, but the land they lived in belonged to other people. Indeed much of it still remained part of the ancestral domain of Amerindians.

Fighting a war for independence had not unified Americans. Rather it created the problem of nationalism—that imperative to hang together once the practical tasks of fighting a common foe and securing a peace treaty no longer exerted centripetal pressure. The commonalities that did exist among the rebellious colonies—language, law, and institutional history—all pointed in the wrong direction, backward to the past, toward Britain, their erstwhile enemy. Ordinary Americans had political identities but they were separate, parochial ones, attached to the vibrant traditions of their own locale. We tend to forget the tensile strength of regional ties, how full of resonating symbols and tactile reminders of a shared past the diverse colonial cultures were. The desire for a closer union, moreover, had not been widely felt, but rather reflected the aspirations of a group of men who were already nationalist in their thinking and cosmopolitan in their outlook. From these leaders came the noisy complaints in the 1780s about state factions and the Cassandra-like predictions of political fragmentation. The Constitution they championed provided new institutions for national governance, but its very success in removing power from local majorities worked against the forming of a popular, patriotic culture. Neither the constitutional debates nor the state ratifying conventions produced the stuff of culture in appeals to cherished sentiments and references to visceral convictions. The case for "a more perfect union" was made in a lawyerly fashion by nationalist leaders, most of them lawyers. Outside of their circles, there were abroad in the land few common sentiments, fewer shared assumptions operating at the intimate level of human experience, and a paucity of national symbols recognizable from Georgia to Maine.

There was the Declaration of Independence with its charged statement of high moral purpose, but its thrilling affirmation of inalienable rights proved far more divisive than unifying in the 1780s and 1790s. The flagrant contradiction between slavery and the principle of equality led to the first emancipation movement as one after another of the northern states abolished slavery in the waning years of the eighteenth century. With these remarkable acts the old surveyor's line that Mason and Dixon had established as the boundary between Maryland and Pennsylvania became the symbolic division between freedom and slavery. This in itself was an ominous development at a time when so few sentimental ties existed to pull Americans into a national union.

The return of prosperity after the postrevolutionary depression also strengthened confidence in the republican experiment, but the conversion of American exceptionalism into a unifying ideology did not take place until the mid-1790s. Then a critical juncture in domestic politics converged with a momentous tidal shift in European affairs. Convinced of the elitist intentions of the government he was serving as secretary of state, Jefferson in league with James Madison set out to alert the body of politically inert voters about the undemocratic tendencies of the Washington administration. This effort began just as news of the execution of Louis XVI reached the United States. Quite unexpectedly the proclamation of the French Republic called forth a new cohort of American radicals, most of them too young to have engaged in the protests against the British. They took up the French cause as their own, finding in the destructive fury of 1793 a confirmation of the portentousness of the moment. The demise of the French royal family turned Europe's great Continental monarchy into a republic, giving ominous substance to the concept of a revolutionary era and a new dispensation for mankind. Here was a narrative that could lift the American War for Independence out of its British frame of reference and turn it into the first act in a universal drama of political liberation. The French embrace of newness, moreover, suggested that the novelties of American society were anticipations of things to come rather than egregious examples of raw provincialism.

The United States could be harbinger, pathbreaker, and model. Many ordinary white male citizens used American exceptionalism to hitch their wagonload of social demands to the rising star of modern revolution. Profoundly alienated from aristocratic European culture, they could relate to this new European vision of a world-transforming future. The fight against Great Britain that conservatives were happy to account a mere war of independence, the new democratic radicals hailed as the first revolution in a revolutionary era.

The French Republic roused political passions in the United States in part because it coincided with the Federalists' determined effort to recapture the homage of their social inferiors through the workings of an energetic central government. The Federalists' defense of conservative wisdom was forthright enough. They made it clear that democracy stopped on Election Day, defending the decorum, formality, even the secrecy, of the Washington administration as necessary for effective governing. Although the Federalists endorsed meritocracy, they stressed qualifications for public office rarely possessed by ordinary men. Theirs would be a sponsored mobility for those who understood the simple prudence of history and common sense. Alas, instead of being attentive listeners, the public had turned teacher. The Federalists' hopes for deference dissolved into a round of public demonstrations in support of republican France's military victories. Political clubs formed in flagrant imitation of the Jacobins, and a dozen Republican newspapers started into existence for the sole purpose of attacking the government.

George Washington's experience illuminates the new situation. Willing in 1794 to expend a part of his considerable political capital to denounce the republican clubs as "certain self-created societies," his voice carried no further than the circles of officialdom surrounding him in Philadelphia. Outside a different logic prevailed. As one radical writer drolly reflected, "had the British succeeded in impressing our minds with a firm belief in the infamy of self creation, we should never have been free and independent."[3]

During these same years, America entered into a period of great commercial prosperity that promoted the construction of roads, the extension of postal services, and the founding of newspapers in country towns. A dense new communication network amplified the resonance of partisan disputes. The control over information and opinions once exercised exclusively by an elite had been wrested away by the articulate critics of that elite. The tactical advantages that had accrued to an upper class small enough for concerted action were overpowered by the mobilization of the popular will through print campaigns. By 1800 the democratic majority in the United States had found their voice, their cause, and their strategy for prevailing at the polls.

This dramatic reconfiguration of social influence precipitated a withdrawal from politics by Federalist families, leaving the issue of national purpose for others to define. Deeply offended by the crass self-assertion of common folk, many conservatives turned their educated refinement into an end in itself, strengthening their ties with the English world that shared their values. The rambunctious politics of the 1790s brought disillusionment to America's first cultural nationalists, men whose nationalist fervor had been nourished by fantasies of American greatness in areas already marked out by the high civilization of metropolitan Europe.[4] They had expected that the free institutions of America would promote literature, science, and scholarship, not noisy confrontations and egalitarian bombast. For them the outburst of revolutionary passion from uneducated men had proven the conservatives right: when the pot boils the scum rises. The abandonment of national politics by these Federalists reflected more than a change of personnel; it was the defeat of a venerable concept of authority. Responsibility for creating a national identity passed down the social ladder.

America's undistinguished citizens—the ones who voted the Federalists out of office—sought affirmation of their values in the celebration of what was distinctively American: its institutional innovations, its leveling spirit, and—above all—its expanded scope for action for ordinary people. To them the idea of American exceptionalism had enormous appeal, for it played to their strengths. Taking up land in the national domain could become a movement for spreading democratic institutions across the continent. Exceptionalism established a reciprocity between American abundance and high moral purposes. It infused the independence and hardiness of America's farming families with civic value, generating patriotic images that could resonate widely without evoking the curse of slavery. The Fourth of July rhetoric of the hoi polloi made clear that American exceptionalism freed them from the elite's embrace of European gentility. To be genteel, one had to accept cultural domination as the price to pay for admission in polite society. For ordinary Americans the country's greatness emerged in a lustier set of ideals—open opportunity, an unfettered spirit of inquiry, destruction of privilege, personal independence—the qualities reform-minded Europeans had already plucked out from the tapestry of American society at the time of the Revolution.

In this analysis I am distinguishing political independence from national identity, the latter dependent on the wide circulation of compelling ideas to create that imagined community that forms a nation. During the nineteenth century, ordinary white Americans ignored the actual insignificance of their political existence and propelled their republic discursively into the vanguard of the march of progress. The propagandists of American democracy breached the geographic isolation of their country by universalizing what was peculiar to Americans: their endorsement of natural rights, their drive for personal independence, their celebration of democracy. What might be construed elsewhere as uninterestingly plebian was elevated by the national imagination to a new goal for mankind. America was the only nation, Richard Hofstadter once wryly commented, that began with perfection and aspired to progress. And American history was written to explain how this could be.[5]

Most of what really happened in the colonial past was ignored because it fit so ill with the narrative of exceptionalism. The colonial settlements had to be presented as the foundations for the independent nation to come, an interpretation similar in logic to interpreting our own times in terms of the aspirations of those who will live in the twenty-second century. Embarrassing facts abounded in the colonial past. Everywhere one looked one found profoundly different concerns engaging the attention of women and men. The exotic cultures of Africans and Native Americans could not be incorporated into American history, for these people's very claims to have culture would have subverted the story of progress. The self-conscious crafters of American identity took great pride in freedom of religion, but the major religious figures of the colonial era, the Puritans of New England, openly embraced orthodoxy—banishing dissidents, whipping Baptists, even executing four Quakers. "Tolerance stinks in God's nostrils," Puritan Nathaniel Ward announced. And so it went with free speech. Congress composed a Bill of Rights guaranteeing free speech, but colonial legislators had been much more likely to jail their critics than to protect their speech. And then of course there was the elaboration of slave codes by colonial legislators. How were those laws to be integrated into the teleology of a peculiarly free people?

All that vibrated with particular meaning in early America was homogenized into elements of a national heritage for heirs as yet unborn. What the colonial period had to offer were a few heroes like Roger Williams and Benjamin Franklin, ancestors worthy of their descendents, and some memorable scenes. A deep forgetting fell over the 20,000 Puritans who came to America to build a city on the hill for the edification of their European brethren. Instead, the inspiring tableau of dozens of humble Pilgrims sitting down to dinner with Pawtuxet Indians in mutual respect and general thanksgiving came to stand in for the whole gallery of disputatous colonists. Patriotic writers set out to explain how autonomous individuals—virtually all male—endowed with a uniform drive for self-improvement and the universal capacity to act independently had filled the American landscape with farms, schools, factories, courthouses, churches, and assembly halls.

We should not take these accomplishments lightly. Reorienting American social values to the twin poles of liberty and equality was a breathtakingly ambitious moral project that required rooting out the pervasive colonial residues of hierarchy and privilege. True heirs of European culture, the American colonists had perpetuated the invidious distinction between the talented few and the vulgar many, making status an important feature of all their institutional arrangements. Democratizing social values became the task of the country's history books. Through them, a depiction of self-activating, productive nation builders was articulated to replace the venerable theory of natural subordination. As John Stephens had rhapsodized in 1787, Americans would have the honor of teaching mankind the important lessons "that man is actually capable of governing himself."[6]

Now two centuries later, this grand narrative stands in the way of a different understanding of our past, one that foregrounds those experiences that were earlier cast into the shadows. The arguments developed long ago for the radicals' attack on aristocratic pretensions have left a residue of assumptions that impair our capacity to respond to the multicultural agenda. Three insistent themes of American exceptionalism need to be examined, each with its own conceptual entailments: the clean slate with its implicit rejection of the past, the autonomy of the individual with its accompanying disparagement of dependency, and the concept of a uniform human nature with its ascription of universality to particular social traits.

Let's look first at the autonomous individual. The United States in 1800 was poised on the eve of a great evangelical movement, but this successful repietizing of American society did not strengthen religious institutions. Like Jeffersonian republicans, American Protestants forgot the past, indifferent alike to the historic church and its traditions. The proliferation of denominations advertised the freedom of religion even as it necessitated a wall of separation between church and state. By the early decades of the nineteenth century, American churches, like male citizens, had been individualized and endowed with rights to life, liberty, and the pursuit of private truths. Meanwhile nature had come to dominate the social imagination of Americans—the nature that Bacon, Newton, and Locke had made orderly, comprehensive, and knowable. Beneath the myriad of surface variety and detail, the natural philosophers had discovered regularities and uniformities of lawlike certainty. Here was a new kind of authority, one that assigned moral worth to those human arrangements that conformed to the objective and irresistible laws of cause and effect. To detach society from the domain of politics and study it as a manifestation of nature, was to alter dramatically the character of social inquiry. With reality as the dispenser of rewards and punishments, a different kind of freedom could be conceived, one that consisted of liberation from artificial arrangements. "What is?" replaced "What ought to be?" as the dominant moral question posed by nature and what Jefferson called "nature's God."

These inferences from the new sciences, familiar to all students of the Enlightenment, had a special conceptual career in the United States. What could only be entertained as theory in Europe could be accepted by sensible Americans as a description of how things actually were. Carriers of an essential human nature, men and women could shed the irrelevant accretions of time and wipe clean the social inscriptions of outworn usages. To speak the language of sociology, an undersocialized concept of man emerged to take the place of that older European figure who had brought the complex tools of civilization to the wilderness. By construing their own liberty as liberation from historic institutions, the enthusiasts of democracy made the United States the pilot society for the world. It was not Americans, but all men, who sought freedom from past oppression. The presumed universality of their values turned them into empirical propositions about human nature.

A philosophy that taught that nature disclosed the moral ends of human life and then read nature as having endowed each man with a right to pursue his own happiness comported well with the actual biases of most Americans. Their natural rights doctrine was both normative and prescriptive. Factually, it taught that all men are the same; philosophically, that all men should have equal rights; but practically only those men who met the liberty-loving, self-improving ideal were freely admitted to the category "all men." When circumstance, failure, disinclination or racial origins raised barriers to taking one's place as a progressive individual, this was read as empirical proof of a failure of fitness. Over time, this language of uniformity turned differences into deviations. Discursively those people who failed to embody established norms became deviants. And if they were denied their rights, it was nature that authored the denial. We can see these assumptions operating most powerfully in relation to minorities and women, but these are but the most conspicuous applications of a principle that confounded a theory of nature for nature itself.

The idea of a clean slate helped create the illusion of a frontier emptied of human inhabitants, a virginal continent awaiting the arrival of potent males, an image that drew a veil over the violent encounters that actually paced the westward trek of Americans. It also denied the force of history, for it is past actions that clutter up the metaphorical slate. The clean slate suggests most powerfully a freedom of choice—the freedom to be the designer of one's own life unaided or impeded by others. Yet there have always been severe limits to this kind of choice in the United States. Clean slates are denied those people whose color or sex has already been assigned a value at birth. Thinking that we create our own identities highlights volition and autonomy and minimizes the categorical force of race and gender in shaping our social existence. Identities partake of a complex two-way relationship between ourselves and others, in which the messages we send out are frequently returned, unopened. The metaphor of the clean slate promotes more than a rejection of the past; it perpetuates the fantasy that we can uncouple ourselves from a genetic inheritance or from our society's cultural coding. Multicultural histories contest these comfortable illusions about choice and autonomy and force us to attend to those life stories that point to different truths.

Twenty-five years ago a new generation of scholars began ferreting out fugitive facts in the American past. Equipped with computer skills, fresh questions, and excellent eyes, they poured over the records of births, marriages, and deaths; they examined probate inventories, land titles, slave purchases, city plats, employment rolls, and tax assessments. From these recondite sources, they ingeniously mapped the patterns of living and dying, marriage and mobility, opportunity and outcome in an earlier America, giving voice at last to those men and women who had been muffled by the celebration of American exceptionalism. Digging away in the public archives, these historians brought to light the tales of frustration and disappointment that had been buried under the monolithic myth of American success. Here too they found the group dependency—that clannishness born of cruel necessity—that nineteenth-century Americans had found so threatening in the "wretched refuse" from Europe's teeming shores.

The undersocialized concept of man of earlier histories ran headlong into the oversocialized concept of men and women whom the new histories turned into repositories of social data. But there was more than an armory for ideological warfare in this new social research. There was also life—Irish, Italian, Jewish immigrants successively occupying and recoding neighborhood cultures; pioneer women spilling the grief of separation into their prairie diaries; freed slaves miraculously reconstituting their dispersed families at the end of the Civil War; Polish housewives juggling their New World opportunities with their husbands' definitions of propriety. Black Americans so long hidden under the blanket rubric of slaves came alive when we met them as the persistent protectors of their indigenous customs or as bold self-liberators (a rather striking contrast to the label, runaway slave).

A cohort of social historians—many of them the children and grandchildren of immigrants, some the great-grandchildren of slaves—turned their dissertation-writing tasks into a movement of memory recovery. Like the Boston Brahmins who formed the caste of gentlemen historians in the nineteenth century, they too found their ancestors in the

American past, but they found them in most unlikely places for historical personages—shop floors, slave quarters, drawing rooms, relocation centers, temperance meetings, barrios, sod houses, rice fields, tent communities.

With social scientific hypotheses to test, scholars could afford to lavish months, even years, calculating the changing proportion of tenant and farmer-owned acreage in selected counties of Iowa or determining the relative fertility of black women in Jamaica, Barbados, and Virginia. Investigating the behavior of groups, often with only names to count, social historians reported their findings as patterns, structures, models, and processes, using norms, modes, and standard deviations to make their points. The importance of the systematic had finally been flushed out of America's historical records. At last we could see a system—or more ominously, the system—categorizing the worth of individuals, controlling access to opportunity, distributing the nation's cultural and economic goods. Social history lifted from obscurity those who had been left behind, excluded, disinherited from the American heritage. It also demonstrated how the functioning of impersonal systems influenced personal lives and challenged the plausibility of human uniformity, a clean slate, and the autonomous individual.

It would be hard to exaggerate the dissonance between history recounted through the doings of the individual—the American Adam—and history reconstructed with the modular units of group experience. Whether the subject was the charter families of Germantown, Pennsylvania, the enslaved Ibos of South Carolina, the Dust Bowl migrants of Oklahoma, or the political leaders of the Progressive era, the story played differently when the actors were approached as members of a group with discernible group destinies. That old familiar tale of the pioneer man alone with his family, or Protestant man alone with his God, or the rights-bearing man alone with his conscience only made sense when one was confident that the individual's virtues were a natural endowment rather than the product of character-molding processes of socialization. Different assumptions critically affect the moral of one's story. When historians depicted autonomous individuals as being in charge of events, blame for failure could be laid at their feet. When the role of society was made conspicuous, it became harder not to assign responsibility for who got what to the institutional arrangements that patterned opportunity.

The conviction that society got to the individual first and stamped her or him with a group identity raised a number of troubling questions about the older belief in universal human traits. Qualities that had been assumed to be natural began to look as though they might possibly be social in origin. The insistence of younger scholars that the experience of women be taken seriously also gave a rude jolt to the presentation as universal of standards that were merely male. Research on women's lives revealed differences that threw into sharp relief the gender-specificity of our social ideals. Perhaps nothing made clearer the exercise of authority in historical scholarship than the exclusive focus on male interests and achievements.

History like literature speaks directly to our curiosity about human experience, but we need concrete details before we can enter into an imaginative encounter with the past. Philip Greven told us that fathers in Andover, Massachusetts, delayed their sons' marrying by barring their access to land.[7] A few statistics about wills, age at marriage, and land conveyances and we could fill in the social reality of parental control and filial submission. The effect of this new capacity to vivify the characteristics of countless mundane lives is moral. It sparks a human connection. There is an enormous difference, for instance, between knowing that there were slave quarters and being able to gaze at a floor plan and calculate living space. What the history of ordinary life delivers is the shock of recognition—my kind is humankind.

These changes in historical scholarship set off more than a rage of anti-Whiggery. At times, it seemed as though recovering the past of ordinary women and men had produced more history than we could consume. We were—and still are—snowed under by an avalanche of information—much of it unassimilable into a coherent national narrative. But that older, lamented coherence had actually come from the European concept of American exceptionalism rather than wide-ranging empirical research. It depended on an induced amnesia and a depiction of the present as always straining toward a destined end. Some critics now see multiculturalism as a threat to the national unity that the older history cemented. Others claim it sacrifices historical knowledge to the achievement of political ends. They do not recognize that the conventional narrative about a new nation conceived in liberty and dedicated to the proposition that all men are created equal—even when affirmed by the eloquence of a Lincoln—is itself a cultural artifact.

Concepts and theories, of course, deliberately obscure the multiplicity of details in real situations in order to highlight significant relationships. But this involves deciding in advance which human lives and whose social enactments will be counted as significant. And this is an act of authority, not research design. Specifically, the idea of American exceptionalism projected onto the United States a future more significant than its past, encouraging a neglect of the historic diversity of the United States in deference to an imagined time when progressive, cumulative, irreversible processes of change would have worn away the variety in human experience.

Closely examined, the objectivity of science is suspect for historians too. Impartiality involves a logic of identity that denies and represses difference.[8] Every one of the determinative dichotomies of our culture: masculine and feminine, WASP and ethnic, black and white, normal-deviant, heterosexual-homosexual has drawn strength from the suppression of the knowledge of the other. Yet when the suppressed particular has been raised to structured consciousness—as in the histories of the diverse groups that compose the United States—knowledge of the nonconforming cases forces out the question, what exactly is there in the other that must be devalued? If deviations actually give evidence of the plentitude of human possibilities, whose purposes are served by employing a language of uniformity and standardization? Without minimizing the real, enviable freedoms that we Americans enjoy, it is not amiss to consider the oppression exercised by an omnipresent cultural model that has carried with it so many mixed messages about the freedom to be different.

Our sense of worth, our well-being, and even our sanity depend on our remembering. But alas our sense of worth, our well-being, our sanity also depend on our forgetting. Remembering and forgetting determine the history we tell. I read a recent editorial on the various national histories of World War II that concluded with this aphorism: "Remember your sufferings, forget your crimes, and you make war. Forget your sufferings, remember your crimes, and you make peace."[9] Nothing is that simple, but those provocative lines point to the historian's inescapable role as moralist. What we attend to in the past will form that restructured memory that we call history, the reservoir of knowledge about human experience that informs our ideas about suffering and crimes, virtues and vices, recordable accomplishments and unworthy happenings. No scientifically based, objective model exists to guide our curiosity. It is we and the cultural milieu in which we think that determine historical significance.

Multiculturalism does not share the postmodernist stance. Its passions are political; its assumptions empirical; its conception of identities visceral. There is no doubting that history is something that happened and that those happenings have left their mark on our collective consciousness. History for multiculturalists is not a succession of dissolving texts, but a tense tangle of past actions that have reshaped the landscape, distributed the nation's wealth, established boundaries, engendered prejudices, and unleashed energies. To look at those aspects of the American past that do not fit into a one-sidedly celebratory account of the nation's origins will require more, not less, rigorous standards of proof, a greater commitment to research, and a superior capacity for analytical persuasion. This does not mean that ideological partisanship—that scholarly equivalent of original sin—will disappear, but rather that the tension between what we as partisans in life wish to believe and what a rigorous and searching examination of evidence forces us to accept is nakedly exposed. Contention is inseparable from creating knowledge. It is not contention we should try to avoid, but discourses that attempt to suppress contention.

As the torrent of statements about multiculturism so noisily proves, knowledge is power. History exercises that power by awakening curiosity, stretching imaginations, deepening appreciation, and complicating one's sense of the possible. We find writing the multicultural history of the United States difficult because we have never rooted our present in our past. Rather we have used the past as a springboard for vaulting into a future that promises liberation from the past, a future of novelties—new nationalisms, new deals, new frontiers, new world orders. Perhaps we can think of multiculturalism as an invitation to look at what has always been there—a cluttered slate of interdependent and highly diverse people shaped by the consequences of five centuries of interaction in the New World. *E pluribus unum* is an ideal; it is not a description of American life in any period. Free of this restricting ideological imperative, we can now set out to recover the historic diversity in our past.

NOTES

1. Durand Echeverria, *Mirage in the West: A History of the French Image of American Society to 1815* (Princeton, 1957), 69; William Short to Colonel William Grayson, June 21, 1787, Short Papers, II, Library of Congress; and Bernard Fay, *The Revolutionary Spirit in France and America,* trans. Ramon Guthrie (New York, 1927), 194.

2. *Les Amities Americaines de Madame d'Houdetot, d'apres sa correspondance inedite avec Benjamin Franklin et Thomas Jefferson,* ed. Gilbert Chinard (Paris, 1924), 56.

3. *Independent Gazetteer,* January 28, 1795.

4. Joseph J. Ellis, *After the Revolution: Profiles of Early American Culture* (New York, 1979), 29–33.

5. Benedict Anderson, *Imagined Communities: Reflections on the Origin and Spread of Nationalism* (London, 1983), 15. I have borrowed Anderson's phrase.

6. [John Stevens], *Observations on government, including some animadversions on Mr. Adams's Defence of the constitutions of government of the United States of America and on Mr. De Lolmes Constitution of England* (New York, 1787), 14.

7. Philip Greven, *Four Generations: Population, Land, and Family in Colonial Andover, Massachusetts* (Ithaca, N.Y., 1970).

8. Iris Murdoch, "Impartiality and the Civic Public," in *Feminism as Critique: On the Politics of Gender,* ed. Seyla Benhabib and Drucilla Cornell (Minneapolis, 1987), 56–57.

9. "The Right Way to Remember," *Los Angeles Times,* January 29, 1992, B6.

5

THE ENLIGHTENMENT PROJECT
IN A POSTMODERNIST AGE

Reflecting on his experiences during an extended visit to the United States, Sir Lewis Namier observed that America was, in certain ways, a large refrigerator that stored British ideas and institutions long after they had been thrown out at home. This was a sophisticate's damning reference to the irremediable provincialism of Britain's former colonies. Like most Europeans who came to the United States not to settle but to unsettle, Namier divested himself of a number of opinions, among them the conclusion that the Enlightenment was dead everywhere, save in America.

In the years that followed this Namierian obiter dictum, the Enlightenment did seem to draw its last breath—even in America. Scholars lost interest in the subject; students got through college without much sense of the dense circuitry of associations connected to the term. No major book has appeared in English on the Enlightenment for more than twenty-five years. Who now reads Carl Becker's *Heavenly City of the Eighteenth Century Philosophers*? In my own field of early America, the republican revision has succeeded in writing the Enlightenment out of the American Revolutionary era, which was once seen as its triumph. Scholars now fight over whether Thomas Jefferson, who penned that quintessential Enlightenment document, the Declaration of Independence, can best be described as a country party man or a classical republican.

But in other quarters, the fortunes of the Enlightenment have decidedly improved. In a wonderfully paradoxical outcome—one of those

This chapter first appeared as "The Enlightenment Project in a Postmodernist Age," Adams Lecture, Department of Classics and Humanities, San Diego State University, San Diego, California. Copyright © 1994 by Joyce Oldham Appleby and the Department of Classics and Humanities, San Diego State University.

unexpected consequences that sustains one's interest in life—an all-out philosophical attack on the Enlightenment tradition has revived interest in the maligned subject itself. The attackers, of course, have been the postmodernists, that amorphous collection of twentieth-century philosophes, literary scholars, science skeptics, and social critics who have joined forces in a comprehensive assault on Western metaphysics, which flowered in the eighteenth-century Enlightenment. This postmodernist campaign has made its presence felt in most disciplines in the humanities and social sciences, not to mention shaking that dozing giant, the American public. And this postmodernist critique of modern knowledge has elicited enough curiosity about the Enlightenment to raise it from the near dead.

Celebrators of irony, postmodernists might consider this the greatest irony of all—the battering they have given to the foundations of modern knowledge has revived interest in modernity. But that is exactly what has happened. In order to understand the philosophical stance of postmodernism, one must recover the modernist canon, which is its target, and retrace the trajectory of modern thought from Bacon through Locke, Hume, Smith, Kant, Hegel, Marx, Nietzsche on to the cascading rivulets of linguistics and structuralism, which brings us to the moment some decades ago when the postmodernists' deconstructive enterprise began. The key is the Enlightenment concept of nature, because the postmodernists' embrace of the social has thrown nature into high relief. This nature that I speak of—in retrospective—can be seen as an invention issuing from the seventeenth- and eighteenth-century natural philosophers who changed nature from a frightening, divinely inspired creation to a grand object of human curiosity—a secular realm of explication and experimentation. Nature seen through Enlightened eyes lost its mystery and acquired instead a fund of facts—realities hidden behind beguiling appearances, which nature would share with the patient reader.

The biggest revelation was order—a dazzling world of cause-and-effect relationships that reason could penetrate. Where the poet saw profusions of particular delights in nature, the Enlightenment hero—the scholar or savant—penetrated this surface of specificity to find the uniformities of natural design. From this discovery of order came the whiff of something even more revolutionary—the principle of universality. Everything worked the same way, despite the variety of shapes, colors, textures, and densities. What was truly important about the elements of nature was their subjection to the same pressures. Uniform forces played on the material of the world in uniform ways, making possible the expression of natural laws. Here was the metaphysics of design, the philosopher's picture of the unvarying ways of nature. It was a picture that no one ever saw because the actual appearances offered to our five senses distorted more than they revealed.

This uniformity would confirm itself through measurement and categorization. In order to see through and beyond the senses to the orderly universe, philosophers elevated the "clear and distinct" idea to a preeminent place in human communication. Through "clear and distinct" ideas observations about nature could be made. Like a floodlight the "clear and distinct" idea shone on the unknowable, throwing into the shadows impressions, intuitions, nonconforming particularities, immeasurable responses to the world—the stuff of poetry. The "clear and distinct" idea also introduced a hierarchy to knowledge as well as a lexicon of discovery, observation, and explanation.

The knowing subject that René Descartes had earlier described became central to the Enlightenment agenda, but this did not lead to an exploration of subjectivity. Rather it prompted an exaltation of the human mind's capacity to mirror nature. Bacon said it first: "God hath framed the mind of man as a mirror or glass, capable of the image of the universal world, and joyful to receive the impressions thereof."[1] And here language, as the essential tool of civilized men and women, was relied on to convey the "clear and distinct" ideas that told about the world as it actually was, that reflected and represented what the mind saw.

Time underwent a transmogrification also. It lost its personal meaning and took on new packaging, parceled out in processes, systems, and developments. Cumulative effects, sequential patterns, and incessant dynamics could be seen flowing into the great river named progress. The contrast, of course, was with the dominant ideas of the old regime, where the golden ages of antiquity and the Garden of Eden had reminded Europeans and Americans that they lived in a fallen state. The classical concept of cyclical change had linked human life to natural growth—at least to the observable cycle of conception and birth, vigorous growth to maturity, inevitable decay, and death. But the new script of improvement took over the imaginative space once devoted to the poignant story of degeneration. To project fresh, constructive change as always lying in the near future was to imagine society poised at the threshold of accomplishment: collective life in a perpetual adolescence.

This favorable attitude toward change transformed the relationship between present and past and present and future: the expectation of positive improvement in the future denigrated both past and present. To a large extent the past lost its attraction and the present became a mere springboard. A host of human problems could be ignored because progress would catch up with them in the future. To look favorably on change, which after all is the dreaded unknown, took a thorough remapping of the cultural terrain. To domesticate the future, as it were, to give people the sense that they knew what was coming, required robust images, for only they could quiet anxiety about the human disasters that had figured so largely in religion and literature. Success in doing this represented an extraordinary reach of human confidence and persuasive power.

From this fresh orientation toward change came the drive for reform—personal reform, social reform, even the reform of nature. Once the belief in progress infected the brain cells of the West, the world as a given to be understood, accepted—even cherished—yielded to the spirit of inventiveness, to the determination to design, improve, and replace. With this endorsement of a restless ingenuity came the unavoidable conclusion that society was a human invention. Could there possibly be a more awesome realization? No longer called on simply to understand God's creation, the savants and scientists took on the task of manipulating that creation, capturing its powers in sluices and boilers, and directing their force toward practical ends.

Human nature—another inventive phrase of the Enlightenment—came to be seen as an endowment, a bundle of potentialities rather than a cast of problematic tendencies like the impulse to sin. Here the Enlightenment drew on the sensational psychology of John Locke, who described the infant human mind as a tabula rasa not too different from Bacon's mirror of nature. Again the comparison cuts sharpest with the reigning assumptions of human corruption, utter dependency, and invariant wickedness collected under the rubric of original sin.

Posited in a different intellectual milieu, the notion of a tabula rasa might have remained locked up in philosophical treatises like the one

Locke wrote, but read alongside the Enlightenment orientation toward positive change, this hypothesis about the infant's openness to first impressions suggested that new experiences might write an alternative story line for the human race. Thus construed, the blank mind of the human child produced the underpinnings for the idea of progress, the most robust of the images that tamed the future for the present.

Implicit in the Enlightenment appeal to reason over reverence was the belief that human beings had a self-regulating mechanism that enabled them to take care of themselves, teaching them why they should restrain their passions for their own good rather than out of obedience to authority. It was called self-interest and like everything else it was a part of a natural law, the law of self-preservation. Integral to these novel ideas about the fundamental human personality had been the observations of people in the marketplace.

Growing with the rapidly increasing complexity of world trade in the early modern period, this commentary put into circulation ideas about the uniformity of human responses. Thus alongside the other contentious discourses about modernity grew up an analysis of economics that pivoted around the new concept of the reasonable man. To reduce the multifarious details of economic life to a set of general laws represented an imaginative leap of great consequence. An impressive mastery was achieved when the evanescent acts of buying and selling were construed as parts of a real, if invisible, process. More important, treating economic activities as parts of a natural order led analyzers to search for the sources of regularity that they found in a predictable human response—self-interest.

Whereas Christian sermons stressed man's degenerate condition ("in Adam's fall did sin we all") and popular drama emphasized the fickleness and impulsive behavior of men and women, economic writers saw constancy and reasonableness in the decisions made in bargaining. In commercial exchanges men and women appeared to be calculating very carefully their own advantage. They sought out the best bargains and generally revealed themselves as dependable and reasonable when prompted by self-interest. From these reflections on human nature, made famous in *The Wealth of Nations*, came the powerful idea of individual autonomy. Adam Smith brought to fruition a century of observations of market behavior with his depiction of the economy as a natural system.

Human beings, inherently disposed to truck and barter, sought their self-interest in market bargains. Their profit-maximizing habits were regulated not by well-crafted laws or wise magistrates, but rather through the competition of other profit-maximizing market participants. As Smith dryly commented, it was not from the benevolence of the butcher and baker that we got our good cheap meat and bread, but rather from their own self-interested drive to secure as much trade for themselves as possible. This ironic logic of nature—the patterned result of unintended consequences—became another of nature's secrets to be explored and exploited.

The reconceptualization of nature, sponsored by Enlightenment enthusiasts, produced the new order's symbiotic relationship with science. Science fashioned its own social milieu, which embraced the qualities of openness, criticism, and experimentation. Scientists relied on accessibility, encouraged dissent, promoted the quest for greater knowledge, replaced divine intention with instrumental reasoning, and offered outcomes as a standard for judgment. However, outside of Great Britain, its American colonies, Switzerland, and the Netherlands, European absolute monarchs and their established churches opposed the radical thrust of the new science and combated it through persecution and repression. This opposition brought to light the deep incompatibility of the natural order that the scientific method disclosed and the unquestioning submission to authority.

In a long, arduous overcoming of the status quo, Enlightenment thinkers battened off nature. Nature delivered an alternative ordering mechanism to customary authority; nature supplied proofs of new propositions about government and society; nature furnished models for reform. Initially blocked in their effort to promote free inquiry, science's new enthusiasts—particularly on the Continent—began to agitate for the removal of the religious and political impediments to the exchange of ideas. Moved by John Locke's idea that human beings were born as blank slates on which the sensual traces of experience wrote out a destiny, they imagined a reformed world where men's (and it usually was just men's) powers of reason would be expanded in order to embellish humankind and open all societies to endless improvement.

When conservatives—attuned to the different rhythms of human beings—opposed the Enlightenment agenda for social engineering based on newly discovered laws of social action, a century-long battle began.

The philosophes' ideas about reform, education, and science became part of a larger war against absolutism. This campaign for the reconfiguration of Western society created the high drama of the Enlightenment: enter the heroes of science, the martyrs of tolerance, the trumpeters of new inquiries to slug it out with the purveyors of superstition, the defenders of privilege, and the oppressors of the unwashed multitude.

This is the conflict that ushered in our modern age; the ur-cultural war that gives us the frame of reference for evaluating the cultural wars of our own time. Men, Voltaire commented, would not be free until the last priest had been strangled with the entrails of the last prince. Women presumably would have to await some further act of desecration. The French Revolution sped up the process.

From rather modest inquiries into the behavior of plants, gases, and the dating of mountains came an avalanche of theories ricocheting from the physical to the social world—the formidable -isms and -tions—positivism, evolution, functionalism, behavioralism, dialectical materialism, and finally modernization itself, a series of totalizing descriptions of the human enterprise rendered as inexorable processes. From the strongholds of the modern West, there was a clear consensus that its knowledge came from the liberation of reason. That knowledge was power because the truths about nature could move the mountains of ignorance that blocked the path to progress.

Indeed, from the Enlightenment perspective, truth and falsehood were stamped on the universe waiting for the discerning discriminator to make the distinction between them public. Like a heat-seeking missile, human curiosity was presented honing in on reality and detonating its protective cover. Completely absent from this account of how the West built its formidable juggernaut of information was the play of human passion, prejudice, power, or reason in the service of the collective ego. And of course with the astounding transformations wrought by science, technology, the market, the vote, and the classroom, conviction followed fast on the heels of hope. Looking back now, we can see that the modernizers created a new form of absolutism, almost as impermeable as that of the old regime. But this is a hindsight that required the bifocals ground by postmodernists.

Early-nineteenth-century European liberals sought to give political expression to the humane affirmations of the Enlightenment. They set for themselves the task of working out institutionally the implications of their new philosophy, but in the United States Enlightenment values became a national creed and more. From the time of Thomas Jefferson's election as president, modern liberal tenets shed their character as philosophical propositions and came to represent for most Americans the face of reality itself.

Simultaneously American nationalism attached itself to an ideological spin-off of the Enlightenment—the idea of a universal destiny for humankind bound up in individual liberation. By the second decade of the nineteenth century, Enlightenment goals had melded with American Protestant and republican themes to form a civil religion for the new nation. Here lies the explanation for the longevity of the Enlightenment in the United States, which Namier had noted. It had become part of the nation's identity. This new collective understanding of the genesis of the nation, and its import for the world, provided the narrative backbone for American historical writing through the nineteenth century and much of the twentieth. Far from explaining national unity, revolutionary histories furnished it. For Americans, democratic nationalism came to represent the principal vehicle of social progress. Blending the intellectual and nationalistic challenges of the Enlightenment, Americans looked at the history of the United States as a great predictor, foretelling the future of the world's oppressed people who would one day throw off the yoke of oppression and come into their full human estate.

The explicit political philosophy of the Declaration of Independence suggested a heroic history in which individuals created government in order to secure their inherent rights. At the time, however, it would have taken a highly imaginative reworking of historical materials to turn the Declaration into the logical termination of America's colonial experience. People who lived through the Revolution knew with what sudden conviction Americans had chosen independence. While hardly novel in its propositions, the Declaration introduced radical affirmations about the basis of government. Its appearance in 1776 represented an unexpected eruption in the thirteen discrete histories of the colonies. Still, if the Declaration were made to appear as the natural end point of colonial developments, then the independence of the United States could be understood as the climax to a long sequence of events that tied the intentions of the first settlers to the fulfilling acts of the Revolution and Constitution. Within a generation, a powerful interpretive tradition had formed that did exactly this.

In successfully shaping historical memory to these ends, personal identity and national identity were powerfully fused. One became an American by exhibiting the autonomy implicit in the natural rights doctrine. Collectively Americans loved their country because it promised to the world—in the words of the Gettysburg Address—"that government of the people, by the people, for the people, shall not perish from the earth." Americans were indeed invested in the Enlightenment project.

In making nature the thread on which to string the central ideas of the Enlightenment, I have tried to show how reform, progress, education, individualism, democracy, science, and human knowledge hung together, coming as they did from the same interpretive matrix. This is a retrospective interpretation, for Enlightenment thinkers did not see their assertions as part of an innovative discourse. These constituted for them discoveries into the nature of the universe itself. More than any other body of social thought, the Enlightenment hid its roots and denied the historical genesis of its convictions. Ranging themselves behind the protective shield of science, modernists, by and large, have resisted seeing the moral and historical components of their worldview. Whether in the study of the elements, the organization of politics, or the rearing of children, Western scholars until very recently insisted on the objectivity of their observations of reality, the neutrality of their findings, and above all the impartiality of their standards. Sustained by prodigious technological advances and spread by the economic and political muscle of Western state power, modernity still continues to impress, everywhere but in its homelands.

If, as Namier said, the Enlightenment had the longest life in the United States, perhaps some law of compensation has determined that with us postmodernism has had its greatest impact. Postmodernism has thrived with us, because here the hollow moral core of mindless change, of deracinated individuals, of nature conceived as a machine is experienced as a social failure. Like the return of the repressed, the scholarly imagination has flooded back to the parched lands of a premodern sensibility. Historians now neglect the heroes of progress in order to reconstruct the diversity disclosed in the past through the lives of ordinary men and women of all races. Feminists have subjected the lexicon of the social and physical sciences to a withering X-ray scrutiny. Deconstructive weapons have been trained on Enlightenment confidence. Postmodernists have bored away at the metaphysical foundations of Western knowledge, destabilizing its language, and exposing the inadequacy of its representation of the human community. Narratives have been scrambled, authors deprivileged, identities fragmented, truth relativized, language clouded, and the operation of reason confined in cultural parameters.

Stringing all the discursive beads of modernity on the thread of nature simplifies the task of naming the lever with which postmodernists moved the mighty modern world: the social. Wherever Enlightenment thinkers found nature in charge, postmodernists have found society, and the perversity of this inversion has served them well.

The first and boldest move came from Michel Foucault, who scorned the naïveté of the Enlightenment belief that the objective, neutral pursuit of knowledge created power. "Knowledge is power," Francis Bacon had said, to which Foucault rejoined three and a half centuries later, "No, Power is Knowledge." Academics can understand this substitution very well. Tenured and empowered by the rules of institutions that grant the degrees and licenses to others, it is our power that speaks when we determine whether our students share in knowledge or tomfoolery. Our networks of associational life only serve to broadcast and confirm our judgments or the collective judgment of our fellow practitioners.

From Foucault came the idea of discourse through which the widest sweep of social power was exercised, and exercised most effectively on the babe born with the blank mind. In the prison, the laboratory, the clinic—we could add the library and seminar room—discourses shaped practice, conferred status, categorized participants. Wishing to expose the Enlightenment faith in the liberating power of reason, Foucault chose to study social institutions like the prison and clinic, which had been sites of reform, where the new tyrannies of individuation and discipline most effectively hid behind the discourse of Enlightenment humanitarianism. The order of things for Foucault was not the complex of cause-and-effect relations that scientists found in nature, but what our hegemonic discourses said it was. For Foucault, social power was all the greater for having an absent creator.

More attuned to the snares of human communication, Jacques Derrida moved the modern world by placing his lever in a different spot. Building on the Saussurian notion of language as a social system, Derrida explored how language frustrates the personal intentions of the language user. For both Foucault and Derrida it is axiomatic that people never mean what they say and never say what they mean. Further, they never know what they are saying and what they are doing by saying what they do. Every text must be deconstructed; the pauses and ambiguities interrogated for the assertions that have been suppressed or the intentions barely visible behind the veil of language. Authors, like children playing with explosives, use words that pack an unsuspected power. And the origin of the power again is society, that disembodied creator of systems of meanings we innocently manipulate. We don't speak language; language speaks us. The medium of expression itself is beyond human control. We play with explosives—in Foucault's analysis, we produce power—or we remain silent. Cruising above the intentionality of the author, now demoted to a language user, the social systems of meaning lend themselves to an infinite array of interpretations. And final meaning can only be deferred.

For postmodernists the most important social element is obviously language. It is through language that everything from our dreams to our career plans acquires meaning. Even the visual field in front of us relies on language for meaning. When we describe what lies in front of us, we marshal the full array of interpretive tools of our society. In this sense postmodernists have applied the word "textuality" to everything that exists in our world. Everything is a text because everything has been socially interpreted. We speak of a particular mountain and we invoke the multiple mountain discourses that range from Mount Sinai through plate tectonics. I found a wonderful example of this in reading a polemical essay from a man whose opposition to Thomas Jefferson was fortified by the twin pillars of Presbyterianism and federalism. "The first ambuscade of Infidelity," Clement Moore wrote, ". . . is among the mountains. Whenever modern philosophers talk about mountains, something impious is likely to be near at hand."[2]

Textuality for the postmodernists explains far more than written documents. It is a concept that highlights the social medium through which all experience comes to us. Gone is the raw encounter with reality celebrated by the Enlightenment and in comes the insidious instruction of society, interpreting the world before we discover it on our own, naming for us its elements while categorizing and codifying, sanctifying and profaning, organizing and energizing. Individuality disappears into the cavern of culture where the walls are fortified by social habit. Given a smart upgrading by postmodernist sensibilities, culture stands where once there was nature as the primordial force in human existence. The idea of social construction pervades the academic landscape in the humanities. We have the social construction of disease, of deviance, of experience, of the sacred, of gender, and most dramatically, of the subject—that subject, the essential thinking man, that once verified existence for Descartes.

The restive intellectual self-liberators of the Enlightenment divined nature everywhere while postmodernists cannot escape the omniscience of the social. Where modern thinkers saw all investigative inquiries converging on verifiable conclusions, postmodernists see inquiries merely proliferating because there is no reality around which they might group. Interpretation has taken the place of explanation. We seek the reasons that socially shaped human beings might hold, not the causes of the realities that impinge on them. All those conceits have disappeared into the limitless vistas of postmodernism.

To render some interim report on postmodernism, we could begin with the enormous contributions that postmodernists have made to our understanding of how knowledge is produced. Their analyses of discourse, language, rhetoric, subjectivity, and intertextuality have carried us a long way into the world where imagination and reality meet. Their radical hermeneutics have teased out suppressed messages. Even their use of confrontational oxymorons and ear-shattering neologisms have helped in the enterprise, implicitly mocking the clear and distinct idea of the impartial reasoning man. They have laid bare the ideological roots of the faith in reason that Enlightenment figures and their nineteenth-century followers either forgot or never knew. Reclaiming the superficial, the particular, and the popular, postmodernists have had wonderful fun with the sober pieties draped around the concepts of fundamental, impartial, and universal.

Many of these themes had been adumbrated earlier by modernist critics, themselves building on a venerable tradition of classical skepticism, but postmodernists went much further, not only deconstructing texts but using the scalpel of deconstruction to scrape against the sinews of social power. Their imaginative and analytical powers have only been matched by their capacity to raise unintelligibility to the level of invective. Flexing a considerable amount of social power themselves, they have rearranged our intellectual and artistic landscape and armed the rising generation of scholars with the daunting vocabulary of self-reflexivity, aestheticization, and all the de-words from deontological to defamiliarize.

Looking at these sequential pictures of the world offered by modernists and postmodernists, we might say that like history, philosophy repeats itself with Marx's addendum, "Yes, first as tragedy second as farce." But I see more continuities than ruptures in these postmodern rifts on the Enlightenment. For me, the postmodernist critique is an extension of the Enlightenment will to know and to live by what one learns. The critical stance that we owe to the Enlightenment has been turned on its makers, a not unexpected development.

It seems quite obvious that knowledge is power and that power is knowledge, that the mirror of nature was more metaphor than possibility, and that the world is both a text and a site of encounters with inhuman objects that are impervious to social discourses. More interesting to me is the revelation, acquired after two decades of postmodernism, that producing knowledge is always an affair of the passions, as captured in the Enlightenment creed: dare to question, dare to learn, dare to tell. Surely this is as appropriate a motto for the postmodernists.

If we can go back to the cave of the Enlightenment after living among the postmodernists, we can maintain that most exhilarating of all intellectual adventures: simultaneously holding contrary positions. To maintain and extend the tensions created by the classical polarities in our world—nurture-nature, subjectivity-objectivity, free will–determinism, tolerance-conviction, continuity-rupture, ethnicity-universality—is to slow the rush to resolution and open ourselves to the complexity and contradiction of the human estate. There would be a cost in such a deliberate refusal to rush to judgment or, to use a postmodernist term, to defer meaning. Richard Rorty has posed the insistent question my recommendation makes salient: Can free societies prevail without the philosophical foundation on which they have rested for two hundred years? Can the Enlightenment project survive postmodernism's exposure of its fantasies? We in the humanities can only observe and note, praise and censure, hope and dread, because we share the human condition of always walking into an unknown future. Indeed, that common fate opens us up to our shared humanity.

NOTES

1. Francis Bacon, *The Advancement of Learning*, ed. William Aldis Wright (Oxford, 1920), 6.

2. [Clement Clark Moore], *Observations Upon Certain Passages in Mr. Jefferson's Notes on Virginia* (New York, 1804), 6.

6

ONE GOOD TURN DESERVES ANOTHER: MOVING BEYOND THE LINGUISTIC: A RESPONSE TO DAVID HARLAN

After historians made that last turn marked "linguistic," they ran into some dangerous curves. Scholarly vehicles were totaled; avenues of inquiry left in disrepair. The timid got out their maps to look for alternative routes to the past; diehards demanded that the dividers be repainted. Some who managed to drive beyond the curves recommended ditching the cars for buses. Fueled by renewable verbal meanings, these buses, they said, add *jouissance* to the trip, even if they never take you where you want to go. David Harlan falls into this last group. Forget the archival loneliness of reconstructing the past, he advises, and fall into a conversation with a dead author.[1] Harlan's witty exposition of the linguistic turn and its implications for historians invites engagement.

Harlan's argument goes something like this: the deconstructionist critique of language exposed a rupture between signifier and signified, leaving the signs that once stood for their union—words—free to change meaning independent of their users' intentions. Among those word users, historians are hit hard. They rely on the stability of word meanings at two points: when they write their interpretations of the past and when they read the texts that serve as evidence of the past. Thus, for historians, the linguistic turn has precipitated an epistemological crisis. Without the bond between signifier and signified, they have no secure language for writing history and no recoverable references in the texts they scrutinize in order to reconstruct the past.

As Harlan readily admits, a long line of skeptics—most of them writing in English—preceded deconstructionists onto the terrain of

This chapter first appeared as "One Good Turn Deserves Another: Moving beyond the Linguistic: A Response to David Harlan," *American Historical Review* 94 (December 1989), and is reprinted with permission.

doubt. Carl A. Becker questioned the notion of a fixed and knowable past in his American Historical Association presidential address of 1932. William James lacked only the word "repristinate" to describe the dubiety of locating the original context of human thought. Even James Madison remarked on the elusiveness of language. In one of the wittiest passages in the *Federalist Papers*, he wrote, "When the Almighty himself condescends to address mankind in their own language, his meaning, luminous as it must be, is rendered dim and doubtful by the cloudy medium through which it is communicated."[2] If these wry reflections about our ability to render intelligible the meaning of others have been around for so long, why have the poststructuralists provoked such anguish in the groves of academe?

Harlan's answer, set forth in some detail, maintains that the poststructuralists have eclipsed the waxing influence of another group of language interpreters, the contextualists. These contextualists, most prominently Quentin Skinner and J. G. A. Pocock, saw in language the entry into a past conceptualist universe. Self-conscious helmsmen, they steered an entire generation of scholars to their tuition of authors' intentions. The contextualists regarded reconstructing the past "as it actually happened" impermissibly empirical, but they held out hope that language was locked into time and place by specific usage. Because of this localization of meaning, they concluded that texts were incapable of moving beyond their particular voices to become part of a transhistorical tradition of canonical works on great themes of Western civilization. Alternatively, the context of social structure was mute about the linguistic means available to historical actors. Class identity offered too few clues about the word games dominant at any one time and place. Informed by this understanding of language encoded through experience, contextualists charted an exciting new scholarly course that avoided the Macphersonian Scylla of Marxist materialism and the Lovejoyean Charybdis of idealist history.

Suggesting that nothing is quite so embarrassing as fighting a rearguard action from the van, Harlan explains how the deconstructionists—Jacques Derrida, Michel Foucault, and Paul de Man, with an assist from Hans Georg Gadamer—have routed the contextualists. With ill-concealed delight, he details the undoing of the contextualists in a few skirmishes, most of them in France. It started with the "death of the author." Then, like modern terrorism, the attack continued through disappearances: "the vanishing text," followed by the knowing subject, the historical agent, the authorial presence, and finally the network of intellectual discourse. Words have become hostage to a new philosophy of language, Harlan tells us, and are no longer available as the building blocks of history.

Harlan does not lament these losses; he yearns for an older form of intellectual history that the contextualists unceremoniously dismissed as naively presentist. With an inadvertent assist from the poststructuralists, Harlan can now make his case for interrogating texts for their possible contribution to the present, regardless of their historical origins. Rather than probe for the writer's intentions, the new ahistorical historian strips old texts of arcane references and outdated foolishness. He or she "reeducates" the ancient author while simultaneously rendering the relevant residue accessible to contemporary readers.

The epistemological crisis has clearly become an invitation to postmodernism for Harlan. If historians yielded up their claim to a monopoly on the past, they could do business with a host of contemporaries interested in narrativity. Disburdened of their task of re-creating old discursive practices, they could freely endorse presentism along with indeterminacy, relativism, and essential absences. Thus unencumbered with disciplinary fixations, they could join literary theorists, deconstructionists, and other liberated readers on a fin-de-siècle romp into the next century.

To all of this I say amen. If we cannot have any theory of knowledge, much less a unified one, let us besport ourselves among the plethora of intellectual delights that knowing subjects can create. But before we eliminate contextualism as one of them, the grounds for dismissal should be revisited. Harlan writes as though the poststructuralists have delivered a knockout punch. By presenting this fait accompli in the form of a report on the poststructuralist critique of language, his proof comes to us as a set of assertions, but, happily, ones that we can easily rebut.

The lynchpin of the poststructuralist argument is that words are no longer captive of the system we call language. Unchained from a fixed referent, words merely point to other words in "the incessant and unremitting play of signifiers." We are told that words form "an endless chain of signifiers in which meaning is always deferred and finally absent." Words, Harlan summarizes, are "protean and uncontrollable."[3] Thoroughly anthropomorphized, words do appear a bit unstable, if not actually giddy. However, to speak of words as being out of control, freed from tyranny, chained to one another, is, if you will excuse the expression, meaningless. Words are totally inert. If they change meanings, it is because some sentient human being has embedded them in a new context that another human being has discerned. Whatever happens to words happens through the imaginative processes of their human inventors and users. Words are protean because human beings use them to explain, encode, describe, mask, obscure, convince, obfuscate, deny, exclude, abbreviate, express, reveal, and tease.

It was exactly this range of human capacities that informed the contextualist intellectual mandate of the 1960s. Aware of the diversity of motives animating word users, they decided that the intentions of authors offered a better guide to the historical meaning of a text than the interests of their class or the relation of the text to some imagined transhistorical discourse. Skinner made the point emphatically: any statement is "inescapably the embodiment of a particular intention, on a particular occasion, addressed to the solution of a particular problem, and thus specific to its situation."[4] The contextualists further asserted, and attempted to demonstrate in their scholarship, that texts were part of a socially created discourse. The intentions of authors were directed and constrained by the authors' conceptual universe as it in turn was constituted by ideological assumptions, rhetorical strategies, and discursive conventions.

The contextualist enterprise, worked out principally in the 1970s, converged with parallel undertakings in cultural anthropology, the sociology of knowledge, and the history of science. For scholars in all these fields, the concept of ideology, referring to socially structured systems of meaning, replaced the more rational and individualistic term "intellectual." Contextualists discovered that the paradigms of social thought giving meaning to words had changed so decisively that historians, like archaeologists, had to dig for past settings of discourse. As Clifford Geertz explained, writing in that innocent pre-poststructuralist time of "Ideology as a Cultural System," the sociology of knowledge ought to be called "the sociology of meaning, for what is socially determined is not the nature of conception but the vehicles of conception."[5] While deconstructionists do not challenge this assertion, they add the caveat deducible from Gadamer's work that, in setting out to determine social meaning and convey our findings to others, we are constituting a new reality, not reflecting a past one. Animated by our own passionate prejudices, we simply add our link to the chain of textual interpretations.

Harlan introduces Gadamer as the author of "a devastating critique" of the hermeneutical project, but Gadamer's argument is a double-edged sword. Gadamer said that historians are embedded in their own historical traditions ("History does not belong to us; we belong to it") and further that the texts they read are themselves a part of an interpretive tradition.[6] This image of successive interpretations, however, is scarcely distinguishable from the successive paradigms in political discourse studied by the contextualists. When Pocock set out to capture the "Machiavellian moment" in England, he was reconstructing one of the many traditions inspired by Machiavelli's writings. Indeed, the idea of interpretive traditions undercuts the claim that words are uncontrollable. Repetition and communication form the essence of a tradition, and neither is assimilable to the notion of protean words dancing away with meaning before the author's ink can dry on the page.

Specific genres generate expectations in readers simply because of the stability of form, of rhetoric, of emplotment. Indeed, to say, as Harlan has Gadamer saying, that we can never recover the tradition in which a text was written but only the tradition of interpretation that has grown up around it raises the logical point of why one recovery is possible and not the other. If we can talk about traditions, why can't we talk about the norms and conventions that give stability to language? If it is not the union between signifier and signified that establishes discursive practices, where are we to look for the structuring force?

A similar out-the-front-door-in-the-back-door maneuver attends the dethroning of authorial authority. After treating his readers to the harrowing orbits of intertextuality, Harlan makes a soft landing by declaring that no one—not even Roland Barthes—"in actual fact" has any trouble telling the difference between great books and comic books.[7] While this is an enormous relief to hear, it throws us back into the domain of reasons, norms, and stable meanings, whose absence created the epistemological crisis in the first place.

In this, as in many places in Harlan's essay, alternatives are overdichotomized. This resembles the logic of an all-or-nothing approach to issues of proof. Harlan's observation that we cannot approach the past "in a state of historical virginity" because of the passionate prejudices that make us human is used to undermine the entire enterprise of re-creating historical contexts. Far better, I would say, to abandon the notion that we can render the minds into a tabula rasa. Elsewhere, Harlan tells us that it is difficult "to continue approaching our texts as objects that *should* be transparent" or to yearn for an encounter with the "now-dead authors in the body of their texts."[8] It is a tribute to Harlan's verbal dexterity that the straw men littering his pages only become conspicuous when picked out of the text.

None of these issues is trivial. The deconstructionists have issued a powerful challenge to that philosophical tradition that asserts the existence of objective truths, considers language a vehicle for the discovery and articulation of those truths, and depends on the stable passage of words from author to reader to spread them. No one reading Derrida or Rorty or Foucault could fail to appreciate the seriousness of the effort to depose this reigning epistemological tradition. The importance of their work, exhilarating, liberating, and cautionary, cannot be exaggerated. However, there is insufficient agreement among these thinkers to undermine our confidence in communication.

Let us consider the question of authorial intention. All of us who write know that we are animated by intentions; further, our intentions, once encapsulated in language, will be comprehended, distorted, elaborated on, and cannibalized by readers. The presence of a vital exchange between author and reader does not eliminate authorial intention, nor does it eliminate curiosity about what those intentions might have been. Similarly, all of us who write know that every other text known to us is a resource—acknowledged or unacknowledged—in our writing. Why should these reflections lead ineluctably to the proposition that intertextuality causes an endless deferment of meaning? Rather, it seems to me, present meaning is not deferred; it stops with every satisfied reader. Only meanings that others in the future might find can be described as deferred.

No logical argument is presented by Harlan, nor have I offered one for my counterassertions. I appeal to experience. And herein lies one of the problems of proof for historians. Physical scientists externalize their validation process through experimentation and demonstration. Many social scientists imitate them by attempting to reduce their investigations to those elements in social life that can be externalized and measured. Humanists cannot follow this path; their validating process involves the assent of a knowing subject. And the knowing subject lives the judgment rather than finds it. Let us take Harlan's claim that "language is an autonomous play of unintended transformations."[9] If I assert in contradiction that only intentional human beings play with words, I must appeal to common experience for proof. Like Barthes's discrimination between great books and comic books, other historians will agree with my statement, but this convergence will follow from our shared practice of doing history at a particular time and place rather than from our commitment to a set of standards abstracted from experience. Can the process through which humanists arrive at common judgments be more adequately explained? If not, is it any the less valid because of its dependence on shared participation in a complex intellectual practice? Perhaps one should not be surprised that lurking beneath battles over words, meanings, and intentions is the archetypal opposition of free will and determinism. By anthropomorphizing words and giving them wings to fly away from human beings, the deconstructionists have created a new set of social forces that impose themselves on human beings. "Words speak people." Turning words into protean, self-animating forces permits us to disregard the troubling issue of human agency. The complex ways that human beings initiate actions, comply with conventions, and dissent from norms can be ingeniously ignored if surrogate forces such as discourse, class, and culture are called on to explain events.

There are really two issues about determinism involved here. One uses the frustration of particular intentions to argue for the insignificance of human intentionality. The claim is, because I cannot control all of the meanings that readers will find in my text, my acted-on intention to write this text is not a causal force. The other stems from a confusion about what causes change. Foucault's claim that discursive practices are subject to abrupt ruptures has encouraged the deduction that changes are independent of human agency, prompted, if at all, by distant, unspecified powers. Yet can anyone doubt that change needs human speakers and writers to introduce novelty and compliant language users to give currency to discursive innovations?

With imagination and opportunity, any collectivity—practitioners of a calling, members of a club, celebrated media figures—can start a fresh language game or shift into a different metaphorical gear. Human beings can even jettison old metaphysical problems, as Rorty has recommended, by ditching the discourse in which those metaphysical problems reside.[10] Innovation need not be a solitary accomplishment in order for human agency to figure in its genesis. Social practices usually change when groups—often cohorts—change, but the plurality of persons does not take away the distinctively human, specifically intentional character of their action. The question then arises (the inevitable regression behind language), How are we to explain when others fail to respond and thus abort a discursive initiative? Engagement with this question will throw us back onto the terrain outside of language, which deconstructionists say does not exist and materialists claim as fundamental.

Language, purpose, power, free choice, determinism—these are the heady words, redolent with meaning and brimming with evocative power that we smuggle into codes and embed in myths. The twenty-first century beckons, and we struggle to respond to its millennial openness by taking stock of our experience. In the beginning, there was the word; in the end, there is tangled intertextuality. The library of human chatter is vast; meanings have been cataloged; expressions checked out and lost. True enough, but do these observations justify eliminating the intending author and the knowing reader from our interpretive quiver? In this endless intertextuality lies the record of human beings talking to and with and behind the backs of one another. We remember but a fraction of it; we must recover all else. Of course, we live and think in the here and now; the question is whether we can re-create any part of the past to keep us company. If the poststructuralists are correct that we cannot fathom the original meaning of the texts offering us a window on other human experience, we will remain imprisoned in the present. Small wonder that historians draw on their practice of reconstructing the past in order to resist this verdict.

NOTES

1. David Harlan, "Intellectual History and the Return of Literature," *American Historical Review* 94 (June 1989): 581–609.

2. Alexander Hamilton, James Madison, and John Jay, *The Federalist Papers*, no. 37 (1787–1788; New York, 1937), 230.

3. Harlan, "Intellectual History and the Return of Literature," 582.

4. Quentin Skinner, "Meaning and Understanding in the History of Ideas," *History and Theory* 8 (1969): 50.

5. Clifford Geertz, "Ideology as a Cultural System," in David Apter, ed., *Ideology and Discontent* (Glencoe, Ill., 1964), 59.

6. Harlan, "Intellectual History and the Return of Literature," 587–88.

7. Harlan, "Intellectual History and the Return of Literature," 597.

8. Harlan, "Intellectual History and the Return of Literature," 588, 592, 602.

9. Harlan, "Intellectual History and the Return of Literature," 596.

10. Richard Rorty, "The Contingency of Language," *London Review of Books* 8 (1986): 3–6.

7

THE POWER OF HISTORY

When I was a college sophomore in 1948, I declared my major in history. I would like to draw on the intervening years to talk about where we have been as a group of scholars and teachers and, more importantly, how we might enhance our influence on our times. This may sound pretentious, but history has an enormous power, and we historians occupy a special relation to it.

I don't think that ours is a time of particularly momentous changes. This old globe and the human race on it have been undergoing dramatic transformations for many centuries. Nor does the coming of the twenty-first century quicken millennial anticipations in me. Still, I am convinced that in good times or bad, critical ones, transitional ones, or normal ones, history can help human beings think better, live more richly, and act more wisely.

I have quoted my favorite lines from Carl Becker at the end of many a discussion, but now I want to begin with them. Confronting his colleagues' adamantine certitude about history's scientific foundations, Becker contended that the value of history was not scientific but moral. "By liberalizing the mind, by deepening the sympathies, by fortifying the will, history," he claimed, "enables us to control, not society, but ourselves—a much more important thing; it prepares us to live more humanely in the present and to meet rather than to foretell the future."[1]

Becker made a critical observation when he differentiated history's moral value from a scientific one: people do not need to understand scientific advances to benefit from them. They might have difficulty telling

This chapter first appeared as "The Power of History" [presidential address before American Historical Association], *American Historical Review* 103 (February 1998), and is reprinted with permission.

a microbe from a speck of dust, but they will recover from an illness as long as their doctors know the difference. The same could be said of social scientific research on recidivism, or teenage pregnancy, or financial forecasting: those who benefit from the knowledge need not understand it. Not so with history. It must be a personal possession to do its work, and we who teach, exhibit, preserve, research, and write history have a responsibility that is measurably different from the scientist's—we must make an intellectual connection with our audiences.

Today we confront a challenge strikingly different from that of Becker's time. The static in our conversation with the public comes not from an inappropriately positivistic view of history, but its very opposite—confusion about the nature of all knowledge and the amount of credibility it deserves. Such bafflement can incite indifference, even antagonism. You can't learn what history has to impart if you start with a false idea of what history is and how historians—amateurs and professionals alike—acquire knowledge about the past. Even worse, without this understanding, you become susceptible to rumors of cultural warfare and academic conspiracies. Doubts about the validity of historical knowledge having been registered with the public, they must be addressed.

I liken the public's consternation about historical knowledge to the epistemological crises that figure in a provocative article by Alasdair MacIntyre.[2] "Epistemological crisis" is a highfalutin phrase for what happens inside our minds when a whole set of assumptions collapses, usually as the result of a startling discovery like the betrayal of a friend or corruption in a trusted institution. At that juncture, MacIntyre explains, we can grab a new set of assumptions as we would a life raft, or we can become more philosophical and reflect on the relation of all presuppositions to practical action. Clearly the introspective response appeals to MacIntyre, prompting him to advance historical narratives as a healer of the damage done, because a historical narrative enables the person—or the field—undergoing the epistemological crisis to explain why the original, faulty assumptions went wrong and then link that explanation to the deeper illumination of how unstated beliefs shore up the reasons we give for our decisions. A narrative that encompasses the sequential steps of unreflective belief, stunned disbelief, and more comprehensive understanding restores the value of human reasoning.

Much of the educated public is having an epistemological crisis about history. They may not be able to put the Thirty Years War in the right century, but they have certainly heard about revisionism. They know that a subject whose very certainty once bored them into the ground has recently begun to shake like the San Andreas fault. Competing accounts of the Holocaust, arguments over the dropping of the atomic bomb, the appearance of Harriet Tubman in school textbooks, descriptions of the demographic disaster that followed Columbus's landfall in the New World, critical assessments of the frontier myth, not to mention talk of deconstruction, decentering, and multiperspectivity, have led to a radical defamiliarizing of their old histories.

Historians, I believe, are an ideal group to undertake the task of explaining to the public how we got from facts to narratives. We are able to do this in part because the processes through which we reconstruct the past are not so remote from everyday thinking. More pertinently, we ourselves have gone through a remarkable period of self-scrutiny that has made us acutely self-conscious of the conceptual underpinnings of history. We have been made aware of the way that language, logic, and social prescriptions affect our scholarship. We have examined our writings as craft, cultural artifact, and vehicle of power. Simple words like "representation," "texts," "interpretation," "genres," "experience," and "perspectives" have taken on Delphic overtones, as we have undergone our own version of an epistemological crisis. Not always comfortable, this working-over has raised consciousness along with ire, turning us into good navigators through choppy intellectual waters. This is what I want to consider here—the course we've recently traveled and how our reflective backward glance might be turned to account in a broader public discussion.

The story covers the discipline's successive engagements, first with the new social history of the 1960s and 1970s, then with the concept of the social construction of reality, and finally with the diffused influences of postmodernism. Different, yet overlapping in time and consequence, the effect of all three has marked a sharp departure from the approach to history that I learned as an undergraduate fifty years ago. More importantly, as I develop in my conclusion, creating a historical narrative of our own epistemological crisis just might enable us to open the public to a history that simultaneously allows us to let go of ossified categories of thought, work through the political uses of the past, and find firm ground in an understanding of how we create our knowledge.

To return for a moment to where I started in 1948: although Carl Becker's skepticism about historical positivism had been widely disseminated—notably in his 1931 AHA presidential address, "Everyman His Own Historian"—when I went to school at midcentury, history texts were still confidently empirical and distinctly godlike with their 360-degree perspective and omniscient voice. Debunking was a favorite classroom entertainment and with the close attention given to dynasties, elections, diplomacy, and war, there was much to debunk. No doubt sophisticated heirs of Becker existed, but they weren't grading my exams.

It was not until the late 1960s after I had received my Ph.D. that I had my first bruising intimation of an epistemological crisis. It came through my husband. When I had returned to graduate school at age thirty-four, my professors had all been considerably older than I. The reverse was true when my husband began working on a doctorate six years later. All of his professors were ten years younger and brimming with Young Turk élan. Eager to share his learning, he brought home news of something called a "model."

"What's a model?" I asked.

"Well, it's the way of making precise your assumptions. You form a model of it."

"Are historians going to start writing about models?"

"It's not a subject; it's a concept in your head."

"Not in my head."

To say that I was furious with this talk of models is to underestimate the anxiety of a freshly minted Ph.D. sensing that she was already out-of-date, moored to a view of history charmingly compatible with saddle shoes and Sinatra swooners.

An essay by H. Stuart Hughes conveys a sense of the profession's zeitgeist in 1963 that I unwittingly reflected. A gem of persuasion, "The Historian and the Social Scientist" is also a historical marker. Hughes had spent a year at the Stanford Center for Advanced Study in the Behavioral Sciences, and with a convert's zeal, he set out to get historians to adopt some social scientific techniques, among them model building. Praising his colleagues for the caution they exhibited toward the metahistories of Oswald Spengler and Arnold Toynbee, he hastened to point out that

there were lower levels of generalization that historians were already using, those implicit in such terms as industrialization or education or revolution. Behind these, he suggested, were models—that word again—that
could be articulated. He went on to recommend quantitative methods—
opinion surveys, sampling techniques, projective tests, content analyses,
scaling that could help historians introduce precision and analytical rigor
to their work. Indeed, Hughes hoped that these arrows in the social scientists' quiver might fell the Hegelian dichotomies that historians favored, making room for gradations and continua.[3]

Social scientists had something else for historians. In their effort to
develop larger and larger generalizations about behavior, they had generated hypotheses, lots of them lying ready for people with the empirical
bent of historians to test: hypotheses about family formation, voting behavior, residential patterning, and electoral cycles. Historical evidence
could be adduced to geographers' hypotheses about the concentric circles of city growth or sociologists' distinctions between sponsored and
challenged mobility.

One can't help being amused (and amazed) at the gingerly fashion
with which Hughes recommended the glories of schematization and
testable hypotheses, knowing that a swarm of quantitative mavens was already poised to turn the discipline upside down with their statistical wiz-
ardry. We can figuratively imagine Hughes in 1963 quickly stepping out
of the way to avoid the crush of graduate students rushing to their IBM
punch cards. The work of these young quantifiers had immediate sub-
stantive, conceptual, and ideological effects. Historians' methods hereto-
fore had focused on evidence, not data, concentrating on how to interrogate dead witnesses or determine the authenticity of documents. Never
before, I think, had historians made explicit the conceptual assumptions
undergirding their research or shown a preference for analysis over description. In doing both, social historians raised the consciousness of the
entire discipline.

The objects of historians' attention changed as well. For years, the
traditional methods of historical scholarship had ruled out research on
ordinary people. Then the synergy of computers and social science techniques supplied the deficiency, proving the truth of Ernest Gombrich's
quip that "where there's a way there's a will." The possibility that something meaningful could be discovered about the unexceptional men and

women of the past stirred the investigative passion of doctoral candidates. Fueled by social curiosity, they strove for a comprehensive knowledge of the past, one in which, for instance, Thomas Jefferson could be rere-membered surrounded by his daughters and grandchildren, the enslaved persons at Monticello, the poor farming families of Albemarle County, and the rank and file of voters who had made him president. Soon the wonderment was how Jefferson and other eminent figures had ever been detached from their lived experience, making us aware of how a partic-ular convention in historical writing—now strange to us—had acquired a taken-for-granted naturalness.

The new social history swept all before it for a decade or more. Its practitioners were brash, bold, and a bit too overconfident of their ca-pacity to refashion the historical record, but they delivered the goods. They put out an "all points bulletin" for missing persons from the past and soon had a squad room full of raffish characters pressing to get into the history books. With a crowd of new figures—working wives, re-bellious slaves, despairing immigrants, striking laborers—clamoring for attention, it soon became clear that, much like uninvited guests at a party, they weren't going to fit in. It wasn't just that the newly re-searched figures weren't dressed properly; they also gave evidence of cherishing values inimical to the ones featured in the familiar account of the nation's steady advance toward "liberty and justice for all." Their lives couldn't be folded into old stories because the old story line was too simple in its linear development, too naive in its celebration of in-dividual achievement, too ideological in its insistence on common na-tional values.

The ideological fallout from longitudinal studies took people un-awares. Investigating the behavior of groups, social historians came up with group figures! They reported their findings through norms, modes, and standard deviations. Quantitative analysis inevitably uncovers pat-terns, systems, and processes. From these artifacts of research it was a short step to the conclusion that the great bulk of American lives had been constrained by such impersonal forces as resource endowments, capital investments, racial preferences, and categorical mistakes like thinking it was natural for women to stay at home. With long-run data sets recorded, scaled, analyzed, and compared, American history ac-quired what had always been rigorously denied—a structure. And there were many structures—affecting education, marriage, longevity, mobility, and opportunity in the American past.

Old forms that had stultified research initiatives could now be breached. One could study slaves as well as slavery, immigrants rather than immigration, laborers, not just unions, and women other than eminent females. While it is true that statistics can imply structures without ever proving their existence, in this case they acted like a lever, moving the American imagination off its individualistic axis. Literally an embarrassment of riches, documentation of the lives of women, workers, farmers, enslaved persons, and Native Americans flushed out a disquieting connection between history and national identity. The nation depended on and expected a tale of social advance, but there wasn't enough success in the fresh stories to merge them seamlessly into this established narrative. Incorporating the new scholarship into the old posed more than a challenge to synthesizing skills; it forced a recognition of the powerful pull of what we might call the metahistory of the country's material and moral progress.

The new social history, with its unsung heroes and documented diversity, dug into the American psyche like a dental hygienist and found a sore spot. What happened to the indisputable facts that had tied the American past to a progressive future? Why wasn't that old social alchemy that had turned diverse ethnic heritages into a unified culture still working? As the anguished cries about the fragmentation of American history bounced off the walls of classrooms and filled newspaper op-ed pages, a question insistently pushed itself to the fore—What lay behind the calls for a unitary history?

Historiographical forces are no more unidirectional than history itself. Although steering in a different direction, the new social history actually reinforced the positivist outlook that Becker had mocked, despite the ideological havoc it wreaked, for it produced a wealth of facts. Moreover, its statistics—arrived at after years of painstaking effort— were often presented standing on their own, as though career patterns, family formation, or voting behavior explained themselves. Without making an effort to discover the human activity behind the statistic, scholars ran the risk of naturalizing existing social arrangements, or they conferred an unthinking legitimacy on the status quo by ignoring the arrangement of power that had produced a pattern. The delight at so many new empirical findings threatened to return history to a new kind of fact mongering.

Moving from information about ordinary people to an understanding of what all this data meant proved difficult as well. Since readers still wanted to know why people acted as they did, tropes from the old national story line were invoked to do the work of interpretation. Occupational mobility was good; immigrant groups that saved for their children's education were more American than those that pooled family wages to buy houses; voting that presaged party formation contributed to the nation's political progress.[4] Some practitioners spoke dismissively of "literary evidence" and demeaned studies lacking a quantitative underpinning as "impressionistic," but, as is so often the case with history, topics that were shoved aside profited from their neglect.

Social history settled into middle age, its disruptive potential spent by the late 1970s, while that old elitist inquiry, intellectual history—transmogrified into the history of mentalite and ideologies—emerged with born-again vitality. Ideology, as a term, lost its Marxist provenance and became the organizing concept for a fresh look at the connection between belief and behavior, rhetoric and reality. In contrast to formal systems of thought, ideologies were seen as mobilizing the emotions while structuring the opinions that generated aversions, enthusiasms, commitments, and prejudices. In its retrofitted form, the concept of ideology enabled scholars to talk about thinking as a social activity. When applied by historians of the United States to the country's nation-building acts of revolutionary resistance and constitution drafting, it revitalized political history. And like the new social history, the "republican revision" of the 1960s directly challenged the venerable assumption that America was born free, rich, and modern.[5]

Ideology soon became the political subset of a more profound historical inquiry that began with the assertion that our sense of reality is socially constructed.[6] This in turn led to a sequence of intensifying questions that has yet to find a resting place. Where earlier disembodied ideas like liberty and class had held sway, now a disembodied society became the matrix for cognition and understanding. Society, in this view, shaped human consciousness, so that any particular structuring of consciousness could be studied as a historical precipitate.

The social dynamics of scientific discovery were made accessible in Thomas Kuhn's *The Structure of Scientific Revolutions,* a book that became something of a social force itself.[7] The power of society to bend nature to its ends focused the insights undergirding women's studies, changing the referent of the word "gender" from a grammatical classification to the cultural elaboration of being female. Soon followed the social construction of disease, deviance, experience, the sacred, and, most dramatically, the subject—the essential thinking man—that once verified existence for Descartes.[8] Scholars began to talk about context as more than an amalgam of economic and social qualities, stressing the persuasive power of paradigms, a word that spread like wildfire through the groves of academe and gave evidence of a paradigm shift in the making.

Despite the heavy emphasis on society, the great German sociologist Max Weber had given a psychological underpinning to the idea of the social construction of reality. All human beings, Weber maintained, had an "inner necessity to comprehend the world as a meaningful cosmos and to know what attitude to take before it." Following this lead, Peter Berger claimed that the "human craving for meaning has the force of instinct."[9] The concept of the social construction of reality thus presumed a human longing that society responded to with its repertoire of myths, sciences, laws, art, and literature—an arresting proposition that someone ought to test.

The muted discussion of such ideas in the 1970s was soon drowned out by the din raised in the 1980s by Michel Foucault and Jacques Derrida. Foucault elaborated a new theory of historical development that replaced the cherished modern mover, the autonomous person, with the postmodern specter of omniscient society exercising a diffuse and pervasive power through discourse.[10] More specifically, Foucault scrutinized the mechanisms through which force had been asserted in the modern period, swooping up the scientific revolution, the law, and humanitarian reform into one conglomerate of social authority. He searched for the hidden organizers of consciousness, the discursive imperatives that controlled both reflection and action. What gave Foucault's ideas their sharp edge was his profound skepticism about all the categories of modern thought—the state, nature, the individual, rationality. For him they became discursive objects to talk about but were never to be given the status of a foundation or an origin. And the social power that intrigued him came not from the men with the bayonets, but from ordinary and unthinking users of those discourses of everyday life that distribute prestige and contempt.

An even more radical skeptic than Foucault, Derrida concentrated his fire on the realist assumption embedded in the Western conviction that words represent reality. Equally suspect to him were the invidious dichotomies of white/colored; male/female; normal/deviant; sacred/profane.[11] The deconstruction of texts—Derrida's perverse method of reading from the margins—offers a way of penetrating their silences and contradictions, but without the hope of a final interpretation because texts for him act more like pinball machines than a safe-deposit box. The slipperiness of words and the unconscious intentions of word users leave all texts open to successive readings. We can see the cherished clarity of philosophers disappear, wrapped in a fog of linguistic ambiguity. Gone too is the raw encounter with reality celebrated by the Enlightenment. In comes the insidious instruction of society, interpreting the world before we discover it on our own, naming and categorizing, honoring and disparaging.

It is in this sense that postmodernists have applied the word "textuality" to everything that exists. Everything is a text because everything has been socially rendered. We speak of a particular mountain, and we evoke the multiple mountain discourses from Mount Sinai through plate tectonics. Textuality for the postmodernists explains far more than written documents. It is a synonym for interpretation, that powerful social instructor. They see language, both in its structure and its specificity, as the means through which human beings confer meaning on a meaningless world. While "death of the author" statements raised eyebrows, the larger point sank in: the authorship of a work is not as helpful in determining how that work acquires sense as is a knowledge of the protocols, rules, and discursive conventions that enable an author to mean something in the first place. Postmodernists have completed the job of placing culture where nature once stood, as the primordial force in human existence.

The postmodern imagination in historical studies followed the social history to the margins of life where one finds the neglected, silenced, eccentric, and transgressive.[12] In these interstices of the historically significant, postmodernists have traced the elusive way that culture serves power. We should accord the movement great respect for turning our attention to the silent workings of human expression and for alerting us to the dense intermingling of interpretation and object in language. Stressing the dispersal of authority through multiple levels of social interaction, they have, however, had less success linking power-generating discourses to any identifiable group. And their contention that it is always power that creates knowledge, not vice versa, ignores the efficacy of Western technology at some risk of credibility.

Flexing their own considerable social power, postmodernists have rearranged our conceptual furniture and given members of the rising generation a dazzling lexical wardrobe with which to clothe their prose. Their analyses of discourse, language, rhetoric, subjectivity, and intertextuality have carried us to the spot where imagination encounters the physicality of the world. Even their use of confrontational oxymorons and ear-shattering neologisms have helped in their enterprise, implicitly mocking the clear and distinct idea of the impartial reasoning man.

Every scholarly movement produces its own waifs. In social history and cultural studies it has been agency. Like all functional inquiries, these have examined the replication of thought and behavior more effectively than the emergence of novelties. They have pinpointed how cultural systems of representation and communication perform, but not why they lose appeal or even take a different turn. To discuss why a discourse no longer satisfies the living would involve us in the interaction of people with their texts and compel us to look at what happens when the texts that constitute reality are challenged by realities outside of them like the joining of the Old and New World. The shift of historical focus from society to culture holds out the promise—as yet unfulfilled—of examining the mechanisms through which social power is exercised. As Karl Polanyi remarked years ago, the fact that a ruling class wishes to rule is an insufficient explanation for its success: "the fate of classes will be much more determined by the needs of society than the fate of society is determined by the needs of classes."[13] The same can be said of discourses.

Historians' recent self-scrutiny has also been informed by some arresting outside critiques of our intellectual practices. Particularly resonant has been Edward Said's exploration in *Orientalism* of how Westerners have dealt with those whom they encountered during a long career of global exploration and military domination.[14] Said's work has inspired an examination of how the other in Western literature has been turned into an essentialized object. Partha Chatterjee and Ashis Nandy have analyzed Western culture from the perspective of the perceiving other. Nandy finds disturbing the U.S. self-image as "a model for the rest of the world, a haven where the poor, the powerless and the discarded of other lands have come and remade their lives voluntarily and produced a culture that now makes transcultural sense." It is "the power of . . . the displaced, the decultured and/or recultured," Nandy writes, "and the public values that can survive in such a society of the uprooted which dominates the global cultural order today." But far from praising this life form of the refugee, Nandy fears its invasive presence and alluring mishmash of secularism, Baconian rationality and incessant, mindless development. Such a culture, he cautions, ensures the decline of community and "the reduction of the person to a fully autonomous, unencumbered individual."[15] Having an enormous partiality for the "fully autonomous individual," I had to read that sentence several times before I grasped its import.

Eastern critics have been particularly astute in assessing how history has shaped Western consciousness. Viewed in the West as a universal form of inquiry, history appears to them as the normalizer of rapid change and a medium of evangelical nationalism. As Prasenjit Duara has explained, Westerners have naturalized the nation-state, making it the container for the experiences of the past. People in the West, he points out, learn history in order to become members of their society: "It is designed to instill pride and/or vengeance for the nation, not to understand the grammar that could question its categories." History teaching is identity formation.[16] William McNeill has made a similar point. History "got into the classroom," he reminds us, "to make nations out of peasants, out of localities, out of the human raw material that existed in the countries of Europe and in the not so very United States as well."[17] Initially tied to the concept of civilization, history glided like a tango dancer into the service of Western nations as they began their ascent to world power.

Thinkers outside the West have helped us see how deeply embedded our categories of thought are in a narrative about human experience that begins with Adam and winds through Adam Smith. Part propaganda and part whistling through the cemetery, national histories have been uniformly proleptic, not just explaining change but normalizing it. They animated the past with anticipation of things to come—capitalism, the nation-state, democracy—robbing these developments of the great complexity of their contingent origins. Our histories have also served as the authoritative documents for judging those people without history.[18] Turning the unique European path into a universal process, they hypostatized a time line for the human race that converted backward into an awesome term.

While Easterners like Nandy wish to emphasize the idiosyncrasy of the West in order to nurture alternative discourses, for us their insights pry loose vestigial assumptions. To naturalize economic developments, for instance, is to move the topic out of the domain of politics and deliver it up to science, just as a naturalized "rational chooser" belongs not to a moral order but to a type of analysis in the social sciences. To stand outside of the filiation of history and the nation-state is not to disparage it, but rather to get some purchase on the powerful presuppositions that have structured our thinking. American historical writing has played no small part in the creation of "the American people." It may once have been important to construe the nation as the holder of the collective experience for our "imagined" community; the trope carries too much baggage to persist.[19] The identity politics of our day have emerged precisely in reaction to the claims of the nation to represent a homogenized people. The challenge now is to think ourselves outside those old categories, not in order to weaken the country to which we give our political allegiance, but to free ourselves from a kind of intellectual bondage.

To return to my original proposition that history has a compelling role to play in contemporary debates: I do not suggest that we sally forth to perplex the public with the conceptual conundrums of postmodernism. Rather I want us to do what historians do very well—act as translators. Indeed we might even say that we have been cultural translators all along, immersing ourselves in that past that is a foreign country in order to sustain our connection to it. We could minister to the confusion and cynicism rampant today by explaining to our audiences how curiosity, interpretation, and culture form the interacting nexus of all knowledge.

There is a pervasive notion abroad in the land that somehow the past lingers on to force the hand of those who reconstruct it. Yet we know that the past as a series of events is utterly gone; only its consequences have infiltrated the present. Some remnants remain like litter from a picnic, but these material leftovers never speak for themselves.

They are inert traces until someone asks a question that turns them into evidence. We need to converse about the vital connection of curiosity and inquiry in scholarship, because one effect of the attacks on Western knowledge has been to popularize a skepticism detached from its critical roots. Ours is a knowledge-dependent society, yet people are quick to believe that knowledge changes in arbitrary ways, even that cabals of like-minded academics exist to poison the well of truth. We live in an age without consensus where paradoxically men and women all over the world are gravitating to the same opinions. History can minister to both perplexities, not only by preserving the endangered diversity of the human experience but also by nurturing an understanding of how learned opinions are formed. Whether we meet our audience gathered in the classroom, at museum exhibits, reading our books, or in public forums, we need to offer an alternative to cynicism by making accessible how we reconstruct the past. And since our work is similar to the construction of all knowledge, learning how historical truths are put forward and tested possesses a protean utility.

We should explain the relation of facts to interpretations. Carl Becker said that historians didn't stick to the facts; the facts stuck to the historians. Yet many of our critics devoutly believe that we could stay out of trouble by sticking to facts—like Julius Caesar's indubitable crossing of the Rubicon. But facts will satisfy neither them nor us. Thousands of people crossed the Rubicon every day; we stick to the fact of Caesar's passage because it is tied to an interpretation of the Roman Republic.[20]

The public is peculiarly nostalgic about historical knowledge and thus repeatedly horrified when historians disturb prior accounts of an event. California textbooks have recently been revised to tell a different story about the Franciscan missionaries and the indigenous people they sought to Christianize, one that describes the effects of the diseases that the friars unknowingly carried north with them. Behind this revision is an active Native American movement and years of painstaking research and scholarly debate about the demographic dynamics set off when Europeans, Africans, and Asians intermingled with Native Americans. A compelling instance of power as knowledge and knowledge as power, the new histories are sure to provoke controversy.

We recognize that curiosity drives research, but we are less certain what drives curiosity. There is much about the past that we do not know and will not know until someone asks a question that leads to that particular patch of material remains. We need to explain that historical knowledge, like all knowledge, is revised because of the new questions driving new research. The same public that hates and fears historical revisions rarely laments revisions in chemistry or medicine which, like those in history, are the result of further investigations, a point that needs sharpening in public.

We could also make more salient the embeddedness of history in the present. A paradox at first glance, the fueling of research by the currency of curiosity makes sense once one gives up the notion that historians operate like vacuum cleaners sucking up scraps from the past. Our common experience with memory helps correct this impression. We know that things have happened in our lives; we know that we retain a selective memory of them, and further that different questions can force us to recover what was forgotten and hence view the whole from a different angle of vision. If we can close the door on the popular view of history as an uninterpreted body of facts, we can open it to the infinitely more interesting issues of how questions lead to knowledge through the mediating filter of culture.

History is powerful because we live with its residues, its remnants, its remainders and reminders. Moreover, by studying societies unlike our own, we counteract the chronocentrism that blinkers contemporary vision. That's why we cannot abandon intellectual rigor or devalue accuracy. History has an irreducible positivistic element, for its subject is real, even if that reality is evanescent and dependent on texts. Historical writing creates objects for our thoughts, making audible what had become inaudible, extracting latent information from the objects that men and women have constructed. This materiality of historical evidence does restrain us. Imagine a willful forgetting of the Holocaust had the Nazis won World War II. Eventually someone would have picked up the trail of clues or stumbled over the contradictions in the documents created by the victors. Texts would then replace texts, but the impetus for the change would have come from the past itself just as scholars reconstructing the succession of post-Columbian demographic disasters had lots of evidence to go on, once their curiosity turned in that direction. The concreteness of history is what gives it the power to compel attention, to stretch imaginations, and to change minds.

Yet historians have altered their approaches to the past. We can take the case of the United States. During the nineteenth century most American history was compensatory, giving to the people an account that justified the country's egregious differences: its relative egalitarianism in a world where privilege was still associated with excellence, its democratic politics in an international order of belligerent monarchies, its heterogeneity at a time when the ideal of a country was to have one faith, one tongue, one ruler, and one set of presumptive ancestors. American history turned the nation's deficits into assets.

This account changed abruptly in the twentieth century when historians took on the role of social critics. In *An Economic Interpretation of the Constitution of the United States*, Charles Beard dragged the Founding Fathers from their pedestals so that their now-demonstrated human frailty might justify new flexibility in interpreting the Constitution. Following Beard's lead, historians located interest group politics in every subsequent era. Over time the Progressives' fascination with class struggles merged with the 1960s' search for neglected Americans. Admirable as this work has been, it has had the effect of prolonging the life of the Progressive paradigm, the earlier summons to muckraking finding an echo in the battle cry of "race, class, and gender."

An enduring part of the Progressives' legacy as social critics has been that few historians have felt comfortable showing capitalism in a favorable light or even in approaching it as a cultural phenomenon of enormous range and fecundity. Far more often, capital and capitalists appear as shadowy presences, or worse as emblems of human rapacity. Although capitalism was the driving force behind Western modernity, scholars have often treated its origins as exogenous. From studies of primitive accumulation to those on advertising-induced consuming tastes, capitalism has been treated as an imposition from outside, disconnected from its cultural roots. Having spent a good part of my life thinking about the human possibilities disclosed by the market economy, I've become convinced that this consensual rendering of capitalism has constricted our capacity to understand the most remarkable organization of human talent in history. The loss is not moral but intellectual—the dozens of research agendas not pursued, not even conceived, because of a reigning ideology.

The complexity of historians' responses to capitalism cannot be laid entirely at the door of an outdated paradigm. There's more to it than that. As R. N. Carew Hunt noted years ago, "For nearly two thousand years European civilization has rested upon a contradiction—between a philosophy and a religion which teach that all men are brothers, and an economic system which organizes them as masters and servants."[21] In the United States this contradiction became more acute because of the emphasis placed on political equality. Looking askance at the European system of inherited status, early-nineteenth-century Americans frequently assumed that economic and political freedom would be mutually enhancing. These quasi-utopian hopes led to inevitable disappointment. And there was much to be disappointed about.

A hundred and fifty years ago, historians exalted the nation's commercial values as proof of democratic vigor; since the Progressives they have focused more on groups that failed to benefit from a profit-driven economy. Perhaps now, as the twenty-first century begins, we may be ready to explore the social complexity of our entrepreneurial system while shedding the celebratory and compensatory burdens of our predecessors.

The power of history is liberating. The past four decades have demonstrated it, if proof be needed. First, social historians located and analyzed group experiences that had been ignored by earlier historians. Then investigations of ideologies and paradigms, followed by postmodernist critiques and cultural studies, plumbed the depths of society's shaping hand in organizing human consciousness through models, discourses, and language's insinuating codes. Today as teachers, exhibitors, preservers, and researchers of the past, we have been forced to think through the acts of appropriation and remembrance. We can no longer plead ignorance of their effects. We're self-conscious about our voices, our genres, our assumptions. If we can live with this indeterminacy, pursue its implications, contend over meaning, give repeated witness to the magnificence of the human effort to understand, and share these acts with the public, we can be certain that history—the quintessential Western discourse—will have no end.

NOTES

1. Carl Becker, *Dial* 59 (September 2, 1915): 148.

2. Alasdair MacIntyre, "Epistemological Crises, Dramatic Narratives, and the Philosophy of Science," *Monist* 60 (1977), 453–71; reprinted in Gary Gutting, ed., *Paradigms and Revolutions* (Notre Dame, 1980).

3. H. Stuart Hughes, "The Historian and the Social Scientist," in Alexander V. Riasanovsky and Barnes Riznik, eds., *Generalizations in Historical Writing* (Philadelphia, 1963), 30, 37, 47–49, 51.

4. James Henretta, "The Study of Social Mobility: Ideological Assumptions and Conceptual Bias," *Labor History* 18 (1977): 165–78.

5. Daniel T. Rodgers, "Republicanism: The Career of a Concept," *Journal of American History* 92 (June 1992).

6. Bernard Bailyn, *The Ideological Origins of the American Revolution* (Cambridge, 1967); Peter Berger and Thomas Luckmann, *The Social Construction of Reality: A Treatise in the Sociology of Knowledge* (New York, 1966); Joyce Appleby, "Republicanism and Ideology," *American Quarterly* (Fall 1985): 1–13.

7. Thomas S. Kuhn, *The Structure of Scientific Revolutions* (Chicago, 1962).

8. Joan Scott, "The Evidence of Experience," *Critical Inquiry* 17 (1991): 773–97.

9. Norman Birnbaum, "Conflicting Interpretations of the Rise of Capitalism: Marx and Weber," *British Journal of Sociology* 4 (1953): 125–41; Peter Berger, *The Sacred Canopy: Elements of a Sociological Theory of Religion* (New York, 1967), as quoted in Rhys Isaac, "Order and Growth, Authority and Meaning in Colonial New England," *American Historical Review* 76 (1971): 730.

10. Michel Foucault, *Madness and Civilization* (New York, 1973); Foucault, *The Order of Things: An Archaeology of the Human Sciences* (New York, 1970); Foucault, *The History of Sexuality,* vol. 1 (New York, 1978).

11. Jacques Derrida, *Of Grammatology*, trans. G. Spivak (Baltimore, 1976).

12. Pauline Marie Rosenau, *Postmodernism and the Social Sciences: Insights, Inroads, and Intrusions* (Princeton, 1992), 8.

13. Karl Polanyi, *The Great Transformation* (New York, 1944), 152–53.

14. Edward W. Said, *Orientalism* (New York, 1978).

15. Ashis Nandy, "Themes of State, History, and Exile in South Asian Politics: Modernity and the Landscape of Clandestine and Incommunicable Selves," *Emergencies* 7–8 (1995–96): 109–14.

16. Prasenjit Duara, "Why Is History Anti-theoretical?" (paper presented at the Center for Chinese Studies, UCLA, May 10, 1997). See also Duara, "Transnationalism and the Predicament of Sovereignty: China, 1900–1945," *American Historical Review* 102 (1997): 1032.

17. William McNeill, symposium at the Library of Congress, March 1–2, 1996, as reported in *Occasional Papers of the National Council for History Education*, September 1996, 1.

18. Vinay Lal, "On the Perils of Historical Thinking: The Case, Puzzling as Usual, of India," *Journal of Commonwealth and Post-colonial Studies* 3 (Fall 1995): 79–112.

19. Benedict Anderson, *Imagined Communities: Reflections on the Origins and Spread of Nationalism* (London, 1983).

20. Carl Lotus Becker, "What Are Historical Facts?" *Detachment and the Writing of History: Essays and Letters of Carl L. Becker*, ed. Phil L. Snyder (Westport, Conn., 1972).

21. R. N. Carew Hunt, *The Theory and Practice of Communism* (New York, 1951), 3.

8

PRESIDENTS, CONGRESS, AND COURTS: PARTISAN PASSIONS IN MOTION

In a fascinating exchange of letters between John Adams and Thomas Jefferson, Adams wrote words that fairly vibrated with alarm, "Elections, my dear sir, Elections to offices which are great objects of Ambition, I look at with terror."[1] A rather startling opinion for a man committed to representative government, it was prompted when Adams read a copy of the new U.S. Constitution that had just been sent from Philadelphia. Both men were on diplomatic missions in Europe, far from the fascinating developments taking place at home. Its provisions for the presidency drew their immediate attention. "A bad edition of a Polish king [they were elected for life]," Jefferson exclaimed. Adams chose to canvass their different reactions: "You are apprehensive the President when once chosen, will be chosen again and again as long as he lives. So much the better as it appears to me."[2]

Having grown to manhood as subjects of George II and George III, Adams and Jefferson could not wholly detach themselves from the referent of a king when they thought about the executive fashioned by the Constitution. However deficient hereditary monarchs might be in other ways, they had solved the transfer of power problem. "The king is dead; long live the king," crowds shouted when death delivered the throne to the heir apparent. Such considerations aroused Adams's fears; their absence marked Jefferson as the democratic iconoclast of his generation.

Elections, as crusty John Adams saw, were the solar plexus of representative government, fragile vessels for performing that political alchemy of turning power into authority. They also diffused lifeblood into

This chapter first appeared as "Presidents, Congress, and Courts: Partisan Passions in Motion," *Journal of American History* 88 (September 2001). Copyright © Organization of American Historians. Reprinted with permission.

democracies. Through them that chameleon sovereign, the people, expressed its will. The United States Constitution, with all its awkward compromises, achieved a certain clarity in the office of the president, the only officer elected by the whole people and answerable to them in quadrennial elections. Only in crafting the mechanism for selecting a president did the convention delegates plunge into another one of their balancing acts.

The handiwork of the Founding Fathers invited searching scrutiny, as Adams and Jefferson demonstrated, if only because they had written a constitution *de novo*, based entirely on the reasoning of fifty-five delegates working without benefit of customary institutions or ingrained traditions. "We love our Constitution because it has been ours for time out of mind," Edmund Burke said about the congeries of precedents that formed the British constitution. No such association with the past ennobled the nine-page document the drafters produced in sixteen weeks of sessions that hot summer in Philadelphia.

During the thirty-six days that the 2000 presidential election hung in the balance, pundits, soothing listeners with the balm of history, frequently referred to the election of 1876. They chose ineptly. The election of 1800 offers a far more illuminating comparison. That of 1876 formed part of the post–Civil War political trauma and sheds little light on the political institutions that were put at risk in November 2000. Contemplating what went wrong in the elections of 1800 and 2000, by contrast, brings us sharply back to the constitutional arrangements for choosing a president. The contrast also throws a spotlight on political parties as the proverbial monkey wrenches thrown into our democratic machinery.

My analysis of the 2000 presidential election begins with the expectations and assumptions that the delegates to the Constitutional Convention brought to the writing of Article 2. Moving into an unknown future, they, like all human beings, had no idea what was in store for them. They did not anticipate the coalescence of political differences into parties nor foresee the pressure that parties would bring to the institutions they had fashioned. After examining the many ways that parties have distorted the drafters' intentions, I will fast-forward to the 1960s and look at the efforts recent presidents have made to free themselves from party control, a development that coincided with the decline of party spirit among voters. In my assessment of the meaning of the unusual climax to the election of 2000, I will try to connect these various threads to an analysis of why a partisan majority on the Supreme Court acted innovatively to end the vote counting in Florida. My analytical comments aren't very tidy, yet exploring the messiness of our recent election bring us face-to-face with the conundrum that the political parties that serve modern democracies by mobilizing majorities also threaten the restraints on power written into constitutions like ours.

The drafters of the U.S. Constitution gave far less attention to the dangers involved in transferring power from one administration to another than they did to creating a president who could exercise independent executive authority. This was the challenge that events of the past few years had made salient to them. Active, populist majorities had moved to the forefront of politics in almost all of the state legislatures during the Revolution. In a general reaction to monarchies, state constitutions had left the office of governor with little more than ceremonial duties. At the same time, the elite leadership in most of the states had yielded to demands for greater representation from their western regions in a bid for wartime support. And finally, men of middling rank who had previously deferred to their social superiors took democratic rhetoric seriously and began to elect men like themselves. Taken together, we have the elements at play in "the critical period" of Federalist imagination: well-organized majorities, all-powerful legislatures, and a populist program of debt relief and tax measures.

The delegates to the Philadelphia Convention quite naturally drew on these immediate experiences as well as older political traditions when they turned their attention to constructing an executive for the nation that they were anxiously bringing into being. Eighteenth-century preoccupations with balance—the balance of power in Europe, England's balanced constitution—acquired new meaning after they had lived through the 1780s and witnessed the vigor of populist politics in the states. These unbalanced state governments, with their swollen legislative powers, had stirred the deepest fears of the gentlemen revolutionaries who, having achieved independence, now wished to put a lid on further social change.

The Constitution restored full executive authority to the office of the president. Going even further, it emancipated the presidential office from both Congress and the Supreme Court. Even the arrangement for the president's selection promoted executive independence with its elaborate scheme of voting for electors who in turn selected the president, if they could form a majority. The president became the only office elected, albeit indirectly, by the nation's collective electorate. The president alone answered to and looked out for the whole people, much as monarchs were expected to do.

When we turn to the Byzantine scheme for electing the president, it becomes even more obvious that ensuring the independence of the office, not the smooth transfer of power from one administration to another, was uppermost in their minds. Without such a relaxed attitude toward presidential succession, they would never have provided for two, possibly even three, elections (if you count a failed Electoral College majority) for selecting the president. One principle, one reservation, and one expectation guided them. The principle: they wanted the president to be independently elected by all the voters. The reservation: they feared direct balloting by uninformed voters. The expectation: that the electors in the Electoral College would push for their state's "favorite son." Hence the provision that electors must cast votes for two candidates, only one of which could be from the elector's own state. So little did the founders expect candidates for president to compete on the basis of ideology that they conceived of the vice president as a runner-up presidential candidate.

What threw all these preparations into a cocked hat was the swift, unmistakable, and enduring appearance of political parties. By the time of the third presidential election, profound political cleavages had rent asunder the collection of disinterested leaders that the public might have expected to stand for president. Party discipline replaced independent voting; in 1800 it was so exact that Thomas Jefferson and Aaron Burr, the Republican candidates for president and vice president, received an equal number of electoral votes, catapulting the election into the House of Representatives, as the Constitution provided for. The Constitution's drafters expected that presidential elections would frequently end up in the House, and the provisions that they made showed their deference to considerations of state power in 1787 instead of long-range thinking about the nation not yet in existence, but so devoutly desired. When the selection of president passed to the House, the Constitution stipulated that the vote shift from the majority principle to "one state, one vote," even though Delaware and Rhode Island then had populations under 70,000 and Virginia contained close to 900,000 people.

A dozen devilishly partisan schemes erupted in 1801 once the choice of president moved from the Electoral College to congressional delegations. Although the two Democratic-Republican candidates roundly defeated their Federalist opponents, their electors' straight-ticket voting turned Jefferson and Burr into competitors for the presidential plum. With Burr willing to play the spoiler, the Federalists had a field day voting on various slates. With four names forwarded to the House (Burr, Jefferson, Adams, and Charles Cotesworth Pinckney), twenty-four different presidential–vice presidential combinations could be voted on! Contemporaries were thrown into a panic, dividing on whether they feared Jefferson's election more than a revolutionary break with the new— hence fragile—constitutional government.[3] Considering the intensity of passions swirling around issues of European war and domestic violence, it is hardly surprising that this virulent partisan campaign prompted ominous predictions about the fate of the United States. Rumors of usurpations and conspiracies had spiced the weeks in which the original voting in the states had taken place. When the tie vote for Burr and Jefferson threw the election into the House, only eight of the sixteen state delegations (Vermont, Tennessee, and Kentucky had now joined the union) firmly supported Jefferson, a bloc insufficient to elect but numerous enough to drag out the balloting for thirty-five rounds. (Thirty-six seems to be the magic number in presidential election turmoil.)

What failed in 1800 with the tie vote was not the Constitution but Congress. Through round after round of balloting, representatives ignored voters' intentions and kept alive a dozen desperate stratagems. Congressional Federalists toyed with such bizarre slates as Adams and Burr and the outrageous reversal of their standard-bearers, Pinckney and Adams. As so often happens at critical moments, someone found the courage to act honorably. In 1801 that someone was James Bayard, Delaware's sole representative and a Federalist, who deferred to the will of the people by withholding his (and his state's vote) from Burr. Just two weeks before the official inauguration day of March 4, Congress named Jefferson president-elect. Asked to explain his motives, Bayard said that he had acted "so as not to hazard the Constitution."[4] He might equally have said that he did not wish to hazard the people's choice. Three years later, Congress proposed and the states ratified the Twelfth Amendment providing for the separation of ballots for the offices of president and vice president. Not men to shy away from realities, America's political leaders recognized that parties had come to stay.

Of course none of this would have happened had the Founding Fathers established the parliamentary system with its prime minister drawn from the legislature. This they emphatically did not do. Perhaps because the "prime" in the title referred back to the king and not forward to the people, the Constitutional Convention rejected such an executive out of hand. I'm not sure that we fully understand this decision, but their rationale for doing so, articulated in the *Federalist Papers*, speaks eloquently of their desire to make officeholders as independent of each other as possible—be they representatives, presidents, or Supreme Court justices. Interestingly, only senators were allowed to remain dependent, working at the behest of state legislatures. Bent on this goal, the Founders reasoned that having independent sources of election would enhance officers' capacity to check one another. Here the differences between the new American nation and Great Britain came into play. Without social classes—the one, the few, and the many of classical republican theory—to do the checking, the Founding Fathers looked to the three branches of government to check each other, as we all learned in civics class. "Ambition must be made to counteract ambition," Madison famously wrote, continuing with the observation that "the interest of the man must be connected with the constitutional rights of the place."[5] The independent executive was not only an end itself; it served as one of several means for checking the tyrannical concentration of power, the bogeyman of eighteenth-century political thought.

This review of the Founders' intentions set my stage for assessing how parties have played havoc with the Constitution and the independence of the president. From the nineteenth century onward, parties grew more powerful and intrusive. Outside the purview of the Constitution, they exercised their influence on the men who wanted or held office. From the party discipline evidenced by straight-ticket voting in 1800 quickly came legislative programs, the distribution of executive patronage, caucuses for selecting candidates followed by formal national conventions with informal, smoked-filled rooms where the deals were done. The sacrifice of officeholders' independence went unnoticed as voters at large found satisfaction in the conviviality of routinized party gatherings. By the twentieth century, political parties were so entrenched in the political practices of the nation that historians and political scientists, like the public generally, unconsciously assumed the "teleology of the two-party system."[6] The United States had developed its own parliamentary system while maintaining the fiction of an independent executive.

Primary elections seemed to give the voters some say in picking their party's standard-bearers, but when Republicans chose the apolitical World War II hero Dwight Eisenhower to head their ticket, they were acting as parties were supposed to. No one could have imagined that changes were in the offing. Yet Eisenhower's successor and vice president, Richard Nixon, took the first step away from America's de facto parliamentarianism. In 1972, Nixon formed CREEP (Committee to Reelect the President), an organization independent of the Republican Party, to secure his reelection. This signaled the beginning of the end for party power brokers. (Just how insubstantial that role became can be measured by the speed of the collapse of the Gingrich Congressional Party.) Simultaneously, voters' job security in the prosperous decades after World War II eroded the vital links of interest that formerly sustained party loyalty.

Starting in the 1970s, one heard less and less about citizens and more and more about taxpayers. The popularity of one issue produced issueless campaigns. While Nixon innovated with a means of liberating the president from parties, Americans in general downgraded the importance of politics in their lives. Presidential candidates took advantage of their independent funds to buy services once supplied by cadres of devoted volunteers. Using mass media, they cultivated the communication values that had audience appeal and tailored their campaigns to the scripting, timing, staging, and financing of the entertainment industry.

If not interrelated in their inception, the two developments of presidential independence and voter apathy had a mutually enhancing force that became evident in 2000. The election foregrounded two campaigners arrayed in tepid opposition to one another—so tepid that the electorate had trouble making up its mind. The overlapping interests of Democratic and Republican donors discouraged discussion of divisive issues, leaving the public bereft of education and direction. With presidents answerable to campaign donors and voters minimally connected to politics, 2000 delivered the inevitable campaign of ennui. Having nothing serious to talk about, political commentary gravitated to personality traits and commercial tactics. America's political indifference curve produced a statistical wonder—a presidential race ending in a dead heat. Only the nefarious balloting in Florida saved the nation from a collective yawn of acceptance. When all thought of anything unscripted, much less unexpected, had become unthinkable, the tallying of the Florida vote finally delivered the excitement that all long-suffering citizen-voter-taxpayers had been yearning for. Day followed day in delicious suspense.

In the election of 1800 people worried about what would happen to the twelve-year-old Constitution. Since then, the United States had become the world's oldest democracy so Americans could relax and enjoy the "the story that kept on giving," brought to them 24/7 on CNN. Elsewhere—within the infamous beltway of Washington, D.C.—the uncertain succession of presidential authority set off alarm bells in what we could call John Adams's intellectual descendents. Out of step, out of line, out of time, a partisan majority of the Supreme Court resolved the immediate question of who won the 2000 election by doing what the Florida Supreme Court refused to do: accept the premature certification of the vote by Florida's secretary of state.

Partisan passions had found a home, of all places, on the Supreme Court. A strange constitutional lodging, but why not? The issues that Americans cared most about in 2000—abortion, school prayer, environmental protection, Miranda rights, worker safety—had already migrated from Congress to the Court. Legislative goals had transmogrified into personal rights in late-twentieth-century America, and blocking judicial appointments had become the political equivalent of bottling up a bill in committee. Rather than legislators declaiming about policy choices to an empty choir, lawyers invoked the First, Second, Fourth, and Fourteenth Amendments to close cases that were more political than juridical. Proof of the court's new partisan importance: when voters threatened revolt because of their Tweedledee and Tweedledum options, friends exhorted them to go to the polls because of the president's power to nominate Supreme Court justices.

Parties played an upsetting role in both the presidential elections of 1800 and 2000, but the resolution of the vote in 1800 strengthened respect for the Constitution, helping it along to its symbolic importance for the nation. Quite the opposite, the Supreme Court's decision in *Gore v. Bush* battered both the Constitution and the Court that the Founders had designed to be even more independent of political pressures than the president.

My analysis sheds light, if at all, on the structural side of the story. The reasons for the personal decisions lie elsewhere. The question lingers: why would five justices prefer to take unprecedented action to foreclose a contentiously close election rather than rely on the resolution process through Congress provided by the Constitution? Perhaps—to put the best face on it—they feared that there would be no James Bayard to rise to the occasion "so as not to hazard the Constitution," or perhaps to put the worst face on it they feared that there would be.

NOTES

1. Adams to Jefferson, December 6, 1787, in Lester J. Cappon, ed., *The Adams-Jefferson Letters: The Complete Correspondence between Thomas Jefferson and Abigail and John Adams* (Chapel Hill, N.C., 1959), 1:214–15.

2. Jefferson to Adams, November 13, 1787; Adams to Jefferson, December 6, 1787, in Cappon, *Adams-Jefferson Letters*, 1:212–13.

3. James E. Lewis Jr., "What Is to Become of Our Government? The Revolutionary Potential of the Election of 1800," in James Horn, Jan Lewis, and Peter Onuf, eds., *The Revolution of 1800: Democracy, Race, and the New Republic* (Charlottesville, Va., 2002).

4. James M. Banner Jr., "James Ashton Bayard: Savior of the Constitution," in Susan Ware, ed., *Forgotten Heroes: Inspiring American Portraits from Our Leading Historians* (New York, 1998), 57–65.

5. *The Federalist*, ed. Edward Mead Earle (New York, 1937), 337.

6. The phrase belongs to Mary Ryan, "Party Formation in the United States Congress, 1789–1796: A Quantitative Analysis," *William and Mary Quarterly* 28 (1971).

9

THE VEXED STORY OF CAPITALISM
TOLD BY AMERICAN HISTORIANS

I n this, the most capitalistic country in the world, scholars have a difficult time making precise just what social relations the word "capitalism" refers to, not to mention how to characterize its development across
the four centuries of American history. Once such taglines as "America
was born free, rich, and modern," "capitalism came in the first boats," and
"only the energetic and ambitious migrated" expressed the shared assumptions undergirding the metahistory of capitalism in the United
States. That story has almost been reversed recently with scenarios about
colonists' traditionalism that could fit under the rubric, "how the new
world has become old and the old world new." Either version is inade-
quate, leaving us bereft of a full understanding of the early Republic. I
believe that the insights of cultural history with its emphasis on recovering past meanings and exploring how men and women communicated
those meanings offers a promising way to reassess the career of capitalism
in America and its conceptual cousins—trade, commerce, and enterprise.

I am approaching "the vexed story of capitalism" as a historical phenomenon, involving the myriad of convictions of those who wrote on
the subject, as well as the theories then available for analyzing the economy. Throughout this discussion I use the term "capitalism" to designate
a system that depends on private property and the relatively free use of it
in economic endeavors. My definition points to the scope of action given
individuals for turning their property into capital by investing in production, an activity usually aimed at returning a profit. It includes legal
protection for hiring labor and selling goods and services in public and

This chapter first appeared as "The Vexed Story of Capitalism Told by American Historians"
[presidential address before the Society for Historians of the Early American Republic], *Journal
of the Early Republic* 21 (2001), and is reprinted with permission.

private. All of this takes place in a culture that rewards enterprise and rationalizes any untoward social consequences as the price to be paid for material advance.

Neither the term nor the system of capitalism figured in nineteenth-century historical writings. That silence came to an end with the 1913 publication of Charles Beard's *An Economic Interpretation of the Constitution of the United States*. This pathbreaking study irradiated a whole new landscape for researchers to dig into. Beard charged that the Constitution was neither a compact of states nor an organic product of American nation building, but rather the work of the Revolution's moneyed leaders, who had grown fearful of democracy. The limited suffrage in 1787, Beard said, had made it possible to rob the people of their political voice. What the Declaration of Independence had bestowed, the Constitution took away. The Federalists' frame of government frustrated future reform too through a Byzantine amendment process. Beard further asserted that holdings in cash, loans, and bonds, not the real property in homes, shops, and farms of most American voters, had united the men who pushed for the Constitution's "more perfect union." He thus separated the economy of commercial agriculture—the capitalism of the many—from the investments of bankers and merchants—the capitalism of the few—choreographing capitalism's entrance into American history through the fancy footwork of an elite aware of its vested interests.

In the compass of a very few pages Beard razed the temple of Constitution worship and erected in its place a peep show that exposed the hidden forces at play at the Philadelphia convention. Newly energized by this tantalizing thesis, researchers in the following decades ferreted out scores of groups in colonial and postindependence America quarreling with each over taxation, debt relief, land banks, paper money, stay laws, price controls, and bankruptcy statutes. Beard was correct: common economic interests created political coalitions. The difficulty came in attempts to connect these groups causally to the major political decisions about declaring independence, ratifying the constitution, or joining the Jeffersonian opposition. Even more discomfiting to the Beardians, the postwar scholarship of Robert and Katherine Brown revealed that a substantial majority of white men in 1787 enjoyed the vote.[1] The electorate that chose the delegates to the ratifying conventions had not been drastically restricted.

Beard's *Economic Interpretation of the Constitution* made the Founding Fathers accessible to twentieth-century readers. In fact, his Founding Fathers were twentieth-century men, their personalities nailed down in a financial statement, their political expertise revealed by their understanding of how property figured in the organization of power. According to Beard, they forged the enduring links between capitalism and the Constitution. Where the filiopietistic histories of the nineteenth century had invoked "the whole American people" as the authors of the U.S. Constitution, Beard disaggregated the people and named interest groups as the movers of events. He went further: "Man as a political animal acting upon political, as distinguished from more vital and powerful motives, is the most unsubstantial of all abstractions," he wrote, even as he was driven by just such political motives to write his masterpiece.[2]

American historians would never again neglect economic forces, nor the marked tendency of industrial capitalism to concentrate wealth and convert that wealth into political power that decisively influenced the Beardians who first analyzed those forces. Early-twentieth-century activists became acutely aware of the contradictions between the free enterprise system and democratic political practices, and they wrote these perceptions into their histories of the early Republic. When they self-consciously set out to revise the record of American nation building, the Progressives hardwired an anticapitalistic bias into U.S. history. Depicted as an inexorable development in a world of modern flux, capitalism acquired the status of a code word. Henceforth it need only be mentioned to conjure up a force that depressed wages, disrupted stable communities, and threw workers and their families onto charity when sickness or age deprived them of strength. Capitalism had entered American historiography by way of a polemic.

The short-lived consensus school of historians, writing in the 1950s, reevaluated Americans' past struggles and concluded that they had been rather tame tussles over the surplus goodies of a bounteous economy. Robert Brown described colonial Massachusetts as a middle-class democracy; David Potter proclaimed "abundance" the most singular feature in American culture; Daniel Boorstin characterized "the pragmatic wisdom" of those who eschewed ideological passions as quintessentially American; and Louis Hartz sketched an unexamined American liberalism sprawling through time, unchecked by either the aristocratic or socialist sympathies found in Europe. Hartz further epitomized the stand of historians as but an "erudite reflection of the limited social perspectives of the average American."[3] Turning the Progressives' anticapitalist bias on its head, those writing history in the 1950s insisted that Americans had always shared capitalistic attitudes. Rather than react to class differences, these consensus historians feared the soul-constricting conformity of American society. They rediscovered Alexis de Tocqueville's *Democracy in America* and turned the "tyranny of the majority" into the most compelling and disturbing truth for their day. They put a rather different spin on the subject of social conflict, but the school didn't prevail long enough to dislodge the Beardian take on capitalism. Even its consensus about consensus owed more to the revelations of the vicious divisions in fascist and communist regimes than to research on the American past.

In the 1960s and 1970s a younger generation of social historians began to raise fresh and searching questions about the details of everyday life in early America. Aided by the new technologies, they became adept quantifiers, using computers to analyze the large data sets found in colonial records. These social historians restored to historical memory a whole world of values and institutions that the original settlers brought with them. No longer did it appear that the United States was born "free, rich, and modern," as Potter and Hartz suggested. Indeed the colonists seemed in some respects even more conservative than the European cousins they left behind.[4] In the recovery of this "world we have lost" lay a new basis for interpreting the force of capitalism in the American past.

Some referred to the cohort of social historians working in the 1960s and 1970s as neo-Progressives because of their concern for ordinary people, but in reconstructing the families and communities of undistinguished men and women, they discovered the settlers' desires to replicate Old World traditions in their New World homes. Despite these different findings, they followed the Beardians in depicting capitalism as an exogenous force, thrust into the lives of unwary folk by profit-maximizing outsiders. New questions, old anticapitalist bias. Where Progressive historians had written out of sympathy with labor in its struggle for union recognition, neo-Progressives focused on a preindustrial period when the contested terrain was not the factory floor, but the green and pleasant countryside where tradition-bound yeomen fought to repel the relentless intrusion of the market.[5]

Anticapitalism had met anti-Whiggery. Now it was out of deference to a traditional way of life that historians decried the steady incursion of commerce and industry in the early Republic. The transition from an agricultural to an industrial economy threatened both equality and liberty as the rich got richer and more and more of America's free citizens, moving from farms to factories, were exposed to the unfreedom of the workplace.[6] History did not disclose the story of progress so much as the process of dispossessing the common people of their most cherished traditions.

Drawing on this work, James Henretta provoked a fresh round of research on capitalism with his persuasive description of eighteenth-century northern farmers as custom-loving patriarchs, hostile to change. Embroiled in a famous controversy with the historical geographer James Lemon, Henretta challenged the consensus idea that the colonists and their early republican successors had been protocapitalists. Beginning with a Beardian definition of capitalism, Henretta dismissed the "calculus of advantage" as a motive in the lives of ordinary northern farmers who, he claimed, strove instead to hold individual ambition in check and abide by customary notions of the proper distribution of work and wealth. Capitalism in Henretta's famous article appears less a historical development than a malevolent conspiracy perpetrated by outsiders to cut through what he called the "web of social relationships and cultural expectations that inhibited the free play of market forces."[7] Articles by Christopher Clark, Michael Merrill, and Robert Mutch inspired a new round of scholarship from Clark, John Brooke, Bettye Hobbs Pruitt, and Daniel Vickers.[8]

Morton Horowitz's *The Transformation of American Law* offered another powerful interpretation of economic development in the promoter-resister mode. Concentrating on legal changes, Horowitz detailed how the judiciary took the lead in shaping the law into an instrument of economic advance cutting against the desires of most American men and women. Through a series of decisions, early republican judges reinterpreted tort law, pushing the cost burden of economic development onto the backs of ordinary farmers and workers while cleansing the common law of its protection of the status quo. Summarizing his review of judicial action in the eighty years after the American Revolution, Horowitz concluded that "law, once conceived of as protective, regulative, paternalistic, and, above all, a paramount expression of the moral sense of the community, had come to be thought of as facilitative of individual desires and a simple reflection of the existing organization of economic and political power."[9]

The judges who transformed American law, Horowitz asserted, were responding to an elite whose entrepreneurial goals ran athwart the conservative sentiments of the bulk of the population. Politicians, happy to have the law's technical language mask policies at odds with the interests of farmers and workers, welcomed the judges' reinterpretation of doctrines affecting tort, trespass, and negligence cases. Although left inferential by Horowitz, the well-being of the vast majority of people was presumed to be in conflict with initiators of economic innovations.

Tony Freyer in *Producers versus Capitalists* divided Americans along axes of size and location. In the cities there were capitalists—bankers, merchants, and members of corporations—who wielded their power through national networks of trade and credit while the rest of the country outside the cities simply produced. Michael Merrill followed a social map similar to Freyer's. For him capitalism in the early republic was inseparable from the moneyed elite while his "agrarian" interest contains working farmers, artisans, and small manufacturers. Merrill argued, like Freyer, that producers became a group-conscious political force, promoting middle-class values as distinguished from capitalist ones.[10]

By far the strongest assertion of popular resistance to the commercial advance that marked the early decades of the nineteenth century comes from Charles Sellers. In *The Market Revolution*, Sellers maintained that "every popular cultural or political movement in the early republic arose originally against the market." Capitalism for Sellers was not a set of economic responses and institutional arrangements oriented to commercial exchanges, but rather a malign and insidious force that fractured families, undermined communities, and uprooted the well-established rural mores enforced by patriarchal authority. Sellers animated this tragic narrative through a series of investigations of religion, family, and politics, each displaying the uneven match between pro and antimarket advocates. Despite the depth and breadth of antipathy to the market in Sellers's account, Jacksonian Americans fought a losing and ironic battle. As he summarized his market revolution's last act, "under the daily pressure of competitive imperatives on participants' lives, every [opposition] movement became a mode of accommodating to capitalist necessity."[11]

While the particular parts of Horowitz's and Sellers's interpretations have not lacked for critics, their more general assertions about an anticapitalist mentality in the early republic have rarely been challenged.[12] Yet evidence abounds that values essential to the rapid and pervasive development of America's internal market flourished in the northern states. The most significant economic changes, particularly in the Jeffersonian era, can be attributed to the congruence between the structural imperatives of economic development and the habits, values, preferences, desires, talents, and predispositions of a sizable proportion of young, white northern men.[13] Freyer's and Merrill's twin differentiation of merchants and manufacturers and national and local markets makes rigid what in fact were extraordinarily fluid boundaries of enterprise.

Undergirding all of these references to capitalism in American historical scholarship have been two powerful theories: one associated with classical economics and one with Karl Marx. The view of capitalism left implicit in American historiography belongs to the Marxist interpretation that stresses the alienation of labor and explains the diverging wealth of entrepreneurs and workers as a consequence of the surplus value of labor that redounds to those who use capital to employ others. The carriers of capitalist methods, in this view, are outsiders—new men—detached from the mores of the rest of the society and propelled forward by their narrow self-interest. For Marx, capitalists represented not only new men, but new men who shared common political goals. With this cohesion, their challenge to the established order precipitated the very class conflict that for Marx operated as the engine of change.

Starting from entirely different premises, classical economists considered capitalism a natural development, proceeding through time slowly until the division of labor revolutionized productive processes. With a greater output to sell, producers had to seek more customers, widen their market, and meet intensified competition with cost cutting. Where Marx had seen the triumph of a capitalist system as a historical phenomenon and traced it to the emergence of a new class, classical economists, taking their cues from Adam Smith's *Wealth of Nations*, placed capitalism in a long sequence of progressive steps that sprang from basic human qualities and evolved over time. Further naturalizing the social, Smith discerned a benign law of unintended consequences when the invisible hand of the market guided self-interested and competitive participants to greater efficiencies for the good of a consuming public.

In both theories economic development is overdetermined, Marx with his dialectical materialism working through class conflict and Smith with the human propensity "to truck and barter" gaining momentum and scope with the "division of labor." Neither theorist showed much interest in the meaning that market participants gave to their activities. Indeed, both theories described developments moving through human beings, not being activated by them. Marx assumed that the capitalists' profit maximizing could force change; Smith's inherent human drives propelled society forward in progressive stages. By universalizing the appeal of a complex social system, classical economists made it difficult to trace the history through which market mechanisms became ascendant. The Marxist approach stifled curiosity in a different way: by asserting that its historical script was inexorable, it left historians with the sole task of assigning parts.

Analysis of human agency in American histories came through other routes. Consensus historians had pushed to the fore the task of figuring out why ordinary colonial voters had repeatedly deferred to their social superiors. Quantifying social historians uncovered traditional mores incompatible with the private initiatives and competitive propensities of market participants. Both puzzles pointed to the need to look at how men and women in the past interpreted their world and assigned— or reassigned—meaning and value to new situations. Here the ideas of the German sociologist Max Weber became apposite. Weber had posed *the* critical historical question of how an economic system, destructive of customary ways, had been able to penetrate the walls of habit that immured men and women living in traditional societies. Most American historians ignored Weber's problematizing of the origins of capitalism when his work appeared in an American edition in 1959, yielding the battlefield of his *Protestant Ethic and the Spirit of Capitalism* to their European colleagues. More recently Stephen Innes, Daniel Vickers, and Margaret Newell have used Weber's work to reexamine commercial initiatives in early New England.[14]

In a further challenge to mechanistic economic doctrines, the Austrian economist Joseph Schumpeter highlighted the crucial leadership of entrepreneurs in replacing outmoded forms of production and marketing. Marx had followed Smith in giving the capitalists themselves a passive role as the recipients of profit in the three-way distribution of returns to labor, land, and capital. Neither saw what Schumpeter did: that money only becomes dynamic through enterprise. From Schumpeter too came the brilliant observation that capitalism involved a ceaseless process of "creative destruction." Just like the questions about voter behavior and the clash of values, these Schumpeterian insights provided an opening for culture. Choice, novelty, selective fit—all played their part in economic development—even as they remained unexamined by American historians more bent on castigating capitalism than understanding its world-transforming dynamics.

Even when scholars' concerns began to shift from production to consumption in the 1980s and 1990s, historians chose the interpretive slant of German sociologists Max Horkheimer and Theodor Adorno of the Frankfurt School, rather than those of Weber and Schumpeter. Here again capitalist development was separated from culture in a critique that defined consumption as escapist buying and commodified leisure—substitutes for authentic experience. In this view, the success of capitalism marked the death of genuine culture while encouraging conformity, passivity, and political indifference among participants-turned-spectators. Other scholars likened market participation to the theater with its reliance on display, if not downright deceit.[15] In these analyses, lower-class consumption has frequently been ascribed to borrowed tastes and manufactured needs. Interestingly, much of the scholarly criticism leveled at past consumption patterns has paralleled the censorious stance taken by contemporary snobs. During the early eighteenth century, Augustan writers wore themselves out attacking the luxuries that their social inferiors embraced, a tack taken a century later by the young Federalists who gathered around Joseph Dennie and filled his *Port Folio* with laments about the Jeffersonian reign of "soul destroying dollars."[16]

But there's hope on the horizon. A new group of European historians has begun to consider buying and spending as cultural activities, opening the way for a reconceptualization of capitalism.[17] Much like Richard Bushman's fine study of consumption directed toward the achievement of refinement, theirs have reimagined what prompted people to spend—even to work harder to be able to spend.[18] Thinking against the anticapitalist grain, they have, as Lisa Tiersten has reported somewhat mockingly, "opposed the view that the advent of consumer culture signaled a fall from grace, a devolution from a world of stable identities and fixed meanings into a landscape of free-floating choices." By showing that commodities are always embedded in social relations and can be invested with a range of meanings from the sacred to the silly, these scholars have recognized that economic life cannot be separated from the culture that invests it with meaning. No purely external treatment of production and distribution can explain the internal world of market participants. Depictions of consumers as victims, they argue, leave readers with "an uncritical nostalgia toward the precapitalist past."[19]

Critical of the "moral and aesthetic revulsion towards contemporary culture," these historians built on earlier work that demonstrated the centrality of consumption in the earliest stages of British capitalist development.[20] Consumers, they suggest, used commodities as modes of expression tied to status, class, occupation, gender, affinities, and individuality. A fine example from the early republic would be David Jaffee's findings about how itinerant craftsmen responded to their rural customers' passion for painted barns, stenciled chairs, and family portraits.[21] The market economy liberated and disciplined them, while involving them in a complex mix of choice and compulsion. Studies of consumption have also revealed the influence of women and children in economic development. As consumption slowly replaced kinship and landowning as primary sources of personal identity, the lines between the public and private were redrawn. Cultural historians have also linked consumers' wonder at new commodities to a heightened curiosity about the material world in general and hypothesized a desire for mastery of that world, leading to interest in education and self-improvement.[22]

My own fascination with the history of economic development began while I was studying publications about trade that emerged in seventeenth-century England. Both the dense circuitry of a market economy and published observations analyzing this new social phenomenon made their entrance simultaneously. My curiosity had been aroused while teaching a course that carried students through the early modern period with readings from Puritan divines to Adam Smith's *Wealth of Nations*. Where, I wondered, did Smith get his view of human nature as fundamentally rational and self-improving? Certainly it bore no relation to the Shakespearean view of giddy, impulsive men and women nor to the Puritans' conviction that "in Adam's fall did sin we all." I turned to these English economic tracts and pamphlets to discover key elements in the colonial worldview.

Through this paper trail, starting in the 1620s and building in volume and sophistication to the 1690s' debate over recoinage, one could trace the intellectual reverberations from new commercial practices. Prescriptions for a favorable balance of trade—a fetish of early modern economic planning—or the impact of coin clipping on inflation rested on expressed convictions about human preferences. Authors tangled up their policy recommendations with assertions about "the natural order of things."[23] Every piece of advice about exchange rates, wages, rents, and account balances called on shared notions about how men and women reacted to choice. Slowly the concept of human behavior that observers gleaned from market exchanges replaced earlier views. These new assertions acquired the status of universal truths, as when Edmund Burke wrote Smith that "a theory like yours founded on the nature of man, which is always the same will last, when those that are founded on his opinions, which are always changing, will and must be forgotten."[24]

These writings convinced me that it took more than the ambitions of a new class of entrepreneurs to leverage a people out of their old ways. Neither did my research confirm Adam Smith's description of how inherent tendencies led naturally to the improvement of economic productivity. Rather I found critics and enthusiasts looking for immediate explanations of the novelties, subversions, pleasures, and disruptions of commerce. Civil unrest in the seventeenth century weakened the political authority requisite for policing economic restrictions. More and more of the English and their colonial cousins seized on enterprise to expand their scope of action and satisfy desires. They innovated and responded to the innovations of others because they could, because they had alternatives. They then construed their economic ventures as part of the larger program of personal liberation linked to representative government and religious toleration. The appeal of capitalism resonated with those who wanted these social changes; its opponents suffered from association with fixed hierarchies and inherited stasis. Important for this reciprocal relation of activity and analysis was the explosive growth of publishing. The rapid dissemination of opinions through print catered to eager, urban readers who were breaking down the barriers between the private and the public.

Disinterring the unexamined assumptions of Marxist and classical economic theory is a necessary step toward building a more adequate analytical framework for reconstructing capitalism's origins in the United States. Unlike the assertions of classical theory, the personal attributes of market bargainers are not universal or inherent, nor can the goals of a capitalist elite explain the receptivity to their initiatives from other social groups. Actual consumers rewarded or punished producers, and they did so in reference to their needs and tastes. The influences at play were multiple. Religion, as Weber showed, could adventitiously promote capitalist-friendly qualities or inhibit them, depending on the faith. Nor did those men and women drawn to novel opportunities know what would be the consequences of their decisions. Even the word "opportunity" has rich connotations, rhetorically construing as favorable openings that some people might find alarming.

Put as pithily as possible, I would name three deficiencies in our historiography: construing as exogenous a cultural transformation that came from within, limiting the appeal of a free enterprise economy to the lure of profit maximizing, and interpreting discrete historical developments as parts of an inexorable process. The movement toward modernity was endogenous, multifaceted, and contingent, yet capitalists appear in our histories as outsiders carrying alien values like so many Trojan horses into the walled communities of the past.[25] The carriers of market cues wear black hats and hoodwink white-hatted farmers and laborers. Similarly the motives for engaging in the array of fascinating activities involved in imagining, making, marketing, and buying commodities has been narrowed to pecuniary advantage while scholars depict consumers too frequently as pathetic followers of advertising mavens or dimwitted materialists. Rarely is the chance to turn money, credit, or labor into capital associated with individual autonomy, readiness for improvement, or the capacity to envision and execute long-range plans.[26] In our histories, capitalist development appears as a deus ex machina, succeeding by force of wealth or the fraud of misrepresentation. Its popular appeal remains unexplored because it is denied in Marxist theory and assumed in classical liberal thought.

There is also a proleptic quality to our explanations of economic growth that reinforces the determinism implicit in the theories. Very much like the acorn-oak analogy, we project the ultimate outcome of every innovation onto the blank slate of the future: the repeal of usury laws leading invariably to Wal-Mart's dislodging mom-and-pop stores. In deciding to produce more for the market in order to achieve a competent security, as Daniel Vickers has argued, eighteenth-century men and women were not opting for the industrialization of the New England countryside. They were moving into an unknown future, weighing alternative courses of action as they went, according to *their* knowledge and values.[27] We have retrospectively created a narrative of advance toward twenty-first century globalization that denies the variety of choices people confronted along the way. Not only does this mind-set distort the play of preferences of successive generations, it obscures the shortsightedness of most people's considerations. Imputing a hidden hand of capitalist destiny to historic developments relieves historians of the laborious task of reconstructing and contextualizing options, but it also robs us of the satisfaction of finding out what really happened.

During the early decades of the twentieth century, American cultural anthropologists broke with the determinism embedded in Darwinian thought. Under the influence of Franz Boas they abandoned universalist theories of evolution in favor of hypotheses about the historical processes that created the particular arrangements of the world's diverse societies. They opened up the vast subject of how human beings have interpreted reality and passed on those interpretations to their young.[28] Through close attention to the details of the societies under examination, the students of Boas put an "s" on the word "culture." Unlike the analysis of society where scholars stand outside their subject looking for objective causes to explain its structure, the anthropologists attempted to get inside a given society in order to capture the perspective of its members.

The Boasian concept of culture has turned out to be the most protean idea of our time, its influence spreading well beyond the scholarly community. With this compelling analytic tool, historians have learned to decode symbols, gestures, body language, and objects, not to mention language itself, attending closely to the multiple media of social communication. The predominance of culture in our current vocabulary has promoted a fascination with the variety of vehicles for sending out messages about how to act, what to think, when to feel. Yet soon after attention to culture spread from anthropology to history, many scholars took "the linguistic turn" and began interpreting cultural products as the covert carriers of oppressive power.[29] They treated tastes, sensibilities, and taboos as tools through which a disembodied society insinuated its coercive authority.[30] From this perspective elites no longer shaped the society, but rather elusive discourses did. The creative processes of change—inventing new forms, refurbishing old institutions—got locked up again, this time in the "prison house of language."[31] While fuzzy at the edges and amorphous in its analytic categories, the older Boasian understanding of culture holds out the best hope for rethinking the origins of capitalism. Its approach to action through interpretations of reality is particularly pertinent to the transformation of our early modern economy with its succession of novelties compelling unrehearsed responses. Because a new system of meaning was in the making, we can see which explanations effectively redirected social energies and which images did the heavy lifting of persuasion. The microscopic scale of most cultural research is here an advantage. The emergent, entrepreneurial economy involved a decentralization of effort, as atrophied central direction yielded to local, private initiatives.

From a cultural perspective, the key issue in the transformation from a traditional to a modern economy lies with the social response to innovation. This is not to say that economic activities are politically neutral. Success in creating new wealth historically has provided leverage for weeding out attitudes and institutions hostile to capitalism, but the dissension that accompanied social change played out through vehicles of meaning not simply machinations of power. Capitalism spawned repeated assaults on authority, not just because of the "creative destruction" that Schumpeter talked about, but also because of its economic enfranchisement of ordinary people, an outreach essential to sustaining growth. Nora Pat Small's study of the struggle over rural architecture in Massachusetts offers wonderful evidence of this dynamic. As they prospered, New England farmers and artisans began adding sheds and shops to their barns, much to the consternation of their aesthetic superiors who wished to see the countryside dotted with rose-covered cottages.[32] In a similar style, we can interpret weaving straw hats and relying on notes of exchange as examples of modernity's assault weapons battering away at preconceived notions of the proper. The accelerated pace of invention and mobility from the end of the eighteenth century onward only intensified the struggle between old and new as people came to terms with a system that rested uneasily on the shifting sands of change.

Capitalism caused a crisis of meaning wherever it acquired sufficient momentum to push aside obstacles to innovation. In these situations, human agency is most salient, for particular persons made the choices that weakened the precepts, rules of thumb, and inhibitions that had regulated behavior. No one path could have been predicted. Nor could any specific set of ideas explain outcomes, for change invariably carried contradictions within it. Agency became a highly charged concept not only because capitalism worked through individual bargainers and decision makers, but also because the idea that members of society were really individuals acting in their own interest served as the principal intellectual support for commercial societies. The early-nineteenth-century economy was never simply a means of providing goods, services, and employment, for it relied on such values and attitudes as much as material resources.

During the past twenty-five years historians writing about early American capitalism have tended to talk past each other, responding to the polemic in the subject rather than its promise of discovery. A common agenda could halt this. The recovery of meaning promises access to motives and, through motives, actions. Reasons, not causes, dominate cultural analysis. Looking for these in research already done could prove exhilarating. Viewed as a cultural, rather than an economic, phenomenon, capitalism can be seen acting as an invisible social engineer. Because it affected access to both wealth and power, its success provoked the outrage of successive groups of moralists, aesthetes, and traditionalists. We don't need to take sides in these battles to do justice to their histories.

Political thinkers in the early republic wrote about free enterprise as a natural ordering device that made limited government possible. Nationalistic fervor also affected discussions of the economy. Growth and prosperity were summoned as proof of the superiority of American institutions. Contemporaries thought that social and economic freedom enhanced each other in an intrinsically American way. Listen to Charles Ingersoll, scion of a distinguished Loyalist family, himself an ardent Jeffersonian: "Where American ingenuity has been put to trial it has never failed. In all the useful arts, and in the philosophy of comfort—that word which cannot be translated into any other language, and which . . . was reserved for maturity in America, we have no superiors."[33]

As historians we are obligated to interrogate the naive views of market boosters like Ingersoll, but we should not minimize the potency of such opinions. By failing to register the popularity of commercial opportunities, we have overlooked the appeal of the market to many of the denizens of rural communities. The conspicuous material advances most men and women witnessed after 1793 cemented an attachment to both the nation and its economic progress. Similarly, the attraction of youth to change, particularly changes that brought them early autonomy, has rarely been studied as a force against traditional economic practices that operated from within communities. The future orientation of the young, as well as their willingness to take risks, even poorly calculated ones, helped commerce overwhelm custom. In all probability the recurring conflicts over innovation waged by conservatives and modernizers were more often clashes between generations than ones between outsiders and insiders or owners and workers.

Capitalism has always been differentially engaging, differentially empowering. Its capacity to create wealth has usually redounded to the benefit of its supporters, but this fact should not stifle our curiosity about how men and women in the past, acting both as producers and consumers, invested new meaning in the lifestyles and careers that this complex system made possible. In the choice to invest, rather than spend, lies the renewable source of fuel for the capitalist engine, but it is culture, not invariant human traits, that shapes choices. Rather than oppose culture and capitalism—as is done in such paired rubrics as print culture and print capitalism—we need to see capitalism as a cultural system.

To turn to the present, the nexus of youth and change, and the economic system that rewarded them both, helps explain why the leaders of the most capitalistic country in the world are always talking about new starts, new deals, new beginnings, and new frontiers. At the same time there is hardly a social ill—the widening gap between rich and poor, the relentless homogenizing of local variations, the corruption of electoral politics—that can't be traced to the incessant innovating in our economic system. As intellectuals, we care about reform and often find capitalism in one of its many manifestations a hydra in its way, but in mischaracterizing the social dynamics of capitalism's origins we handicap ourselves, both as historians and reformers. The rest of the world identifies capitalism's potent mix of institutions and ideologies with the United States. Yet we have relied on German sociologists, Austrian economists, and British empiricists to give it a genuine history. Perhaps with a refurbished concept of culture, we can reclaim the story of the most significant "ism" in our past. And who better to start this intellectual effort than historians of the early republic.

NOTES

1. Robert S. Brown, *Middle-Class Democracy and the Revolution in Massachusetts* (Ithaca, N.Y., 1955).

2. As quoted in Max Lerner, "The Constitution and Court as Symbols," *Yale Law Journal* 46 (1937): 32.

3. Brown, *Middle-Class Democracy*; David Morris Potter, *People of Plenty: Economic Abundance and the American Character* (Chicago, 1958); Daniel Boorstin, *The Americans: The Colonial Experience* (New York, 1964); and Louis Hartz, *The Liberal Tradition in America: An Interpretation of American Political Thought since the Revolution* (New York, 1955), 29.

4. See Joyce Appleby, "A Different Kind of Independence: The Postwar Restructuring of the Historical Study of Early America," *William and Mary Quarterly* 50 (1993). See chapter 2.

5. Allan Kulikoff, "The Transition to Capitalism in Rural America," *William and Mary Quarterly* 46 (1989), reviews the debate. Although the term "yeoman" did not figure in contemporary documents (see Appleby, "Commercial Farming and the 'Agrarian Myth' in the Early Republic," *Journal of American History* 68 [1982]), historians of the early republic have been loath to give it up.

6. See Karen Orren, *Belated Feudalism: Labor, the Law, and Liberal Development in the United States* (Cambridge, 1991), for an exploration of this development.

7. James A. Henretta, "Families and Farms: Mentalite in Pre-Industrial America," *William and Mary Quarterly* 35 (1978); James Lemon, "Comment on James A. Henretta, 'Families and Farms: Mentalite in Pre-Industrial America,' with a reply by James A. Henretta," *William and Mary Quarterly* 37 (1980); and Henretta, "Families and Farms," 20.

8. Christopher Clark, "The Household Economy, Market Exchange, and the Rise of Capitalism in the Connecticut Valley," *Journal of Social History*, 1979; and Clark, "The Household Mode of Production—A Comment." Michael Merrill, "Cash Is Good to Eat: Self-Sufficiency and Exchange in the Rural Economy of the United States," *Radical History Review* 3 (1976); and Robert E. Mutch, "Yeoman and Merchant in Pre-Industrial America: Eighteenth-Century Massachusetts as a Case Study," *Societas* 7 (1977); Clark, *The Roots of Rural Capitalism: Western Massachusetts, 1780–1860* (Ithaca, N.Y., 1990); John L. Brooke, *The Heart of the Commonwealth: Society and Political Culture in Worcester County, Massachusetts, 1713–1861* (Cambridge, 1989); Bettye Hobbs Pruitt, "Self-Sufficiency and the Agricultural Economy of Eighteenth-Century Massachusetts," *William and Mary Quarterly* 41 (1984); and Daniel Vickers, "Competency and Competition: Economic Culture in Early America," *William and Mary Quarterly* 47 (1990). See also Kulikoff, "Transition to Capitalism in Rural America."

9. Horowitz, *The Transformation of American Law* (Cambridge, 1977), 253. See also Appleby, "The Popular Sources of American Capitalism," *Studies in American Political Development* 9 (1995).

10. Merrill, *Producers versus Capitalists: Constitutional Conflict in Antebellum America* (Charlottesville, Va., 1994), 13–16, 24–25, 35, 55; and Merrill, "The Anticapitalist Origins of the United States," *Review* [Fernand Braudel Center] 13 (Fall 1990): 469. See also Merrill, "Putting 'Capitalism' in Its Place: A Review of Recent Literature," *William and Mary Quarterly* 52 (1995).

11. *The Market Revolution: Jacksonian America, 1815–1846* (New York, 1991), 208, 236.

12. See, for instance, Gary T. Schwartz, "The Character of Early American Tort Law," *UCLA Law Review* 36 (1989); William Gienapp, "The Myth of Class in Jacksonian America," *Journal of Policy History* 6 (1994): 232–59; and Daniel W. Howe, "The Market Revolution and the Shaping of Identity in Whig/Jacksonian America," in Melvin Stokes, ed., *The Market Revolution in America: Social, Political and Religious Expressions, 1800–1880* (Charlottesville, Va., 1998).

13. Freyer, *Producers versus Capitalists*, 13–16, 24–25, 35, 55; Merrill, "Anticapitalist Origins of the United States," 469. See Joyce Appleby, *Inheriting the Revolution: The First Generation of Americans* (Cambridge, 2000).

14. Stephen Innes, *Creating the Commonwealth: The Economic Culture of Puritan New England* (New York, 1995); Vickers, "Competency and Competition: Economic Culture in Early America"; Margaret Newell, *From Dependency to Independence: Economic Revolution in Colonial New England* (Ithaca, N.Y., 1998). Naomi Lamoreaux has also addressed these issues in an unpublished paper, "Accounting for Capitalism in Early American History: Farmers, Merchants, Manufacturers, and their Economic Worlds." See Appleby, "Value and Society," in Jack P. Green

and J. R. Pole, eds., *Colonial British America: Essays in the New History of the Early Modern Era* (Baltimore, 1984), 290–316, for a discussion of Weber's earlier, more diffuse influence.

15. Works that compare the market and theater are Jean-Christophe Agnew, *Worlds Apart: The Market and the Theater in Anglo-American Thought, 1550–1750* (Cambridge, 1986); and Mike Featherstone, "Perspectives on Consumer Culture," *Sociology* 24 (1990): 5–22.

16. William C. Dowling, *Literary Federalism in the Age of Jefferson: Joseph Dennie and the Port Folio, 1801–1812* (Columbia, S.C., 1999), 15.

17. Lisa Tiersten, "Redefining Consumer Culture: Recent Literature on Consumption and the Bourgeoisie in Western Europe," *Radical History Review* 57 (1993): 119. See also Colin Campbell, *The Romantic Ethic and the Spirit of Modern Consumerism* (Oxford, 1987), 25ff.; and John Brewer and Roy Porter, eds., *Consumption and the World of Goods* (London, 1993).

18. Richard Bushman, *The Refinement of America: Persons, Houses, Cities* (New York, 1992). See, for instance, Lorna Weatherill, *Consumer Behaviour and Material Culture in Britain, 1660–1760* (London, 1988); and the essays in Brewer and Porter, *Consumption and the World of Goods.*

19. Tiersten, "Redefining Consumer Culture," 119, 135–36. See also Margaret Jacob, *Scientific Culture and the Making of the Industrial West* (Oxford, 1997).

20. Tiersten, "Redefining Consumer Culture," 119–20. See Neil McKendrick, "Home Demand and Economic Growth: A New View of the Role of Women and Children in the Industrial Revolution," in McKendrick, ed., *Historical Perspectives: Studies in English Thought and Society in Honour of J. H. Plumb* (London, 1974), 187–202.

21. David Jaffee, "One of the Primitive Sort: Portrait Makers of the Rural North, 1760–1860," in Steven Hahn and Jonathan Prude, eds., *The Countryside in the Age of Capitalist Transformation: Essays in the Social History of Rural America* (Chapel Hill, N.C., 1985); and Jaffee, "Peddlers of Progress and the Transformation of the Rural North, 1760–1860," *Journal of American History* 78 (1991).

22. Tiersten, "Redefining Consumer Culture," 125, 134–35; and Daniel Miller, *Material Culture and Mass Consumption* (Oxford, 1987).

23. Joyce Oldham Appleby, *Economic Thought and Ideology in Seventeenth-Century England* (Princeton, 1978), 158–70, 199–216, 242.

24. As quoted in R. D. Collinson Black, "Smith's Contribution in Historical Perspective," in T. Wilson and A. S. Skinner, eds., *The Market and the State: Essays in Honour of Adam Smith* (Oxford, 1976).

25. See notes 7, 9, 13, and 14 for exemplary texts.

26. A brilliant exception is Thomas Haskell, "Capitalism and the Origins of the Humanitarian Sensibility," *American Historical Review* (1985); reprinted in

Thomas Bender, ed., *The Antislavery Debate: Capitalism and Abolitionism as a Problem in Historical Interpretation* (Berkeley, 1992).

27. Vickers, "Competency and Competition: Economic Culture in Early America." See also Robert F. Dalzell Jr., "The Rise of the Waltham-Lowell System and Some Thoughts on the Political Economy of Modernization in Ante-Bellum Massachusetts," *Perspectives in American History* 9 (1975): 239–68.

28. Franz Boas, *The Mind of Primitive Man* (New York, 1911); and Boas, *Anthropology and Modern Life* (New York, 1928); Ruth Benedict, *Patterns of Culture* (New York, 1934); and Margaret Mead, *Coming of Age in Samoa* (New York, 1928). See also Clifford Geertz, *The Reinterpretation of Culture* (New York, 1973); and Victoria E. Bonneli and Lynn Avery Hunt, eds., *Beyond the Cultural Turn: New Directions in the Study of Society and Culture* (Berkeley, 1999).

29. Joyce Appleby, "One Good Turn Deserves Another: Moving beyond the Linguistic: A Response to David Harlan," *American Historical Review* 94 (December 1989).

30. Winfried Fluck, "The Modernity of America and the Practice of Scholarship," in Thomas Bender, ed., *Rethinking American History in a Global Age* (Berkeley, 2002).

31. Joyce Appleby, Lynn Hunt, and Margaret Jacob, *Telling the Truth about History* (New York, 1994), 202–17.

32. Nora Pat Small, "The Search for a New Rural Order: Farmhouses in Sutton, Massachusetts, 1790–1830," *William and Mary Quarterly* 53 (1996).

33. Charles Ingersoll, *A Discourse Concerning the Influence of America* (Philadelphia, 1823), 24.

INDEX

ABOUT THE AUTHOR

Joyce Appleby, professor emerita at University of California, Los Angeles, has long taken an interest in bringing history to a larger public. Past president of the Organization of American Historians, the American Historical Association, and the Society for Historians of the Early American Republic, she has thought deeply about the complex relationship of the American public with the country's professional historians. As codirector of the History News Service, she now encourages historians to write op-ed essays for newspapers, showing how the past has influenced the contemporary issues that trouble us.

Her research on the seventeenth and eighteenth centuries in England, France, and America has focused on the impact of an expanding world market upon the way people understood and talked about their society. In her work, she has stressed that a revolution in social theory accompanied the revolution in economic activity.

"Government officials rarely want a robust, honest national history, yet this is exactly what we all need to be effective citizens," Appleby has said. In her career as a historian of the founding era in the United States, she has worked to promote an understanding of the past that can help Americans deal more sanely with the present.

Made in the USA
Coppell, TX
28 March 2023